WHAT HAPPENS IN
AMERICA

WHAT HAPPENS IN AMERICA

ARJUN PANCHAL

Notion Press

Old No. 38, New No. 6
McNichols Road, Chetpet
Chennai - 600 031

First Published by Notion Press 2017
Copyright © Arjun Panchal 2017
All Rights Reserved.

ISBN 978-1-947202-03-0

Contents

PART II: USA AND ITS CHARM

ACKNOWLEDGEMENTS

Never imagined, I would write a novel! But the astonishing experiences with my friends and family influenced me to weave them into a beautiful fiction. My heartfelt thanks goes to:

My editor Rana Rines; artful and amazingly talented professional. Her understanding of Indian culture blended with her editing skills made the novel more entertaining. My sister-in-law Chinki who helped me with her valuable suggestions and fixing the errors.

My mentor Prashant Hemnani, who actually brought my dreams into reality. Vishal Dhundale for being extremely cooperative.

My dad and my uncle Jagdish Vishwakarma for taking risk of their hard earned money on me. My mommy who is ever worried for me for no good reason. My brother and sisters for always cheering me up.

Dearest Yashita with whom I experienced the best college time. My well-wisher Tanya who supported me at each stage staying away.

My wonderful friends who were the rich source of ideas: Kushal, Pratik, Abhiniti, Stephanie, Amit, Neel, Karan, Nitin, Prerna, Ankur, Ronak, Vininder, Vasu, Ruoyi,

Zia, Balaji, Hanu, Mihir, Malvika, Siddharth, Manish, Sundar, Sujith, Jimmy, and many more.

The Notion Press: Karthik, Malavika, Mridula, Jessie, Naveen, Editors, Cover designer and the entire team for selecting and bringing the novel from MS word to book shelves.

And my beloved readers who have picked the book and prepared themselves for an amazing virtual ride to America!

YEAR 2010

THE RUN BEFORE FLY

I had never run this fast in my life. Had it been an Olympic sprint, I would have won the gold medal. I was running late. It was not just for any interview, but an interview for the US visa. Yes – a United States visa interview!

We reached the US Consulate. I asked her to sit in the waiting room. I entered the interview lobby where I was faced with a blast of Arctic air as soon as I walked in. The only reason I could think of for why anyone would keep a room so bone-chillingly cold was to balance out the palpable tension in the room. Of course, there is good reason for this tension. The US visa interview is so unpredictable that even God cannot predict what the outcome will be.

I found a seat in the center of the room and squeezed myself between a nervous college student and a boisterous family of nine. As I waited for my number to flash on the screen, I found that there were three very distinct categories of people. The first came away dancing, evidently on cloud nine, while leaving the window because they had passed the interview. Others were not so lucky and their sagged shoulders told the sad tale of rejection. The third category – people like me – felt like we were in a scary movie, just waiting to find out who the killer was. It almost felt like we were waiting for the killer to come creeping up from behind. The longer we waited, the more fear and anxiety filled the icy room. I felt my blood racing through my veins, and began counting my heartbeat to distract myself from the terror I felt. Suddenly, my heart seemed to skip a beat. My number was flashing on the board. I shot up from of my seat, and clutched my belongings to my chest for comfort. I took a deep breath and headed for the window where my interviewer was waiting. He was blond and handsome, I think, and sort of stoic and beefy-looking. He was the first American I'd ever talked to in my life.

"Hey, how you doing, today?" asked the officer. My eyes drifted down to the plaque on his desk. I saw that his name was Todd.

"I am very well, sir. How are you?" I replied, trying to be as boisterous as I could to suggest that I was confident, though I fear it may have come off as a little desperate.

"Pretty good, thanks! So why do you wanna go to the States?"

"Sir, to do my MBA."

"Interesting. And which university will you be attending?"

"University of Massachusetts, Boston," I said confidently.

"How many universities did you get accepted to?"

"Yes," I replied, with that same high level of confidence.

"Yes what?" He asked as suspicion smeared across his face.

I realized I didn't understand the question. He spoke so quickly and I was not used to deciphering the American accent so fast. "Pardon?" I asked with a smile plastered to my face. Must maintain confidence!

"How…many…universities…did you get accepted to?"

"Oh! Sorry! I misunderstood you. Three…three universities."

"And how long are you planning to stay in the United States?"

"I will come back after my graduation and will join my family business."

"Hmm."

I couldn't tell from his facial expression if I was giving him the answers he was looking for. At that moment I really wished I'd been taught how to read a poker face. Micro-expressions, I think that's what they're called. But I hadn't, and my brain was racing. Should I say something else? Should I call him by his name and try to win him over with one of my charming stories? Just as I was about to launch into a story about the time I accidentally ate a piece of plastic fruit, he looked down at my passport and started writing. I stopped myself from speaking. With each word he wrote, my heart pounded harder, growing heavier with each beat. He looked up at me blankly. My breath went shallow as I waited for him to say something…

PART I

LIFE ON A MOTORCYCLE

YEAR 2004

1

ENGINEERING AND THE ILLUSION OF HARD WORK

Indore

Every teenager going off to college builds up in his head the anticipation of a new lifestyle of independence and all of that begins with the first step on campus. I was going to specialize in Information Technology. I pursued this not because I liked it, but because, at that time, there was a rush to get into IT and it seemed like the best chance for a return on my investment. I had gotten into a decent engineering school in Indore, so I already felt pretty good about myself. My confidence was high, and I envisioned campus life with pretty girls by my side and the cool and popular guys I would befriend. What I never asked myself was, "Do I really want to do Engineering?"

On that first day, there were several information booths set up to help us navigate our new environment. Thankfully, I spotted a kiosk dedicated to helping students find housing. I meandered over, and there I met two other students, Raghav and Kabeer, who were also looking for roommates. They seemed to be quite nice and innocent, so we decided to live together, and a week later, the three of us moved into a one-bedroom apartment.

Our apartment was located on the fourth floor of a large building with no elevator. We lived on crap and crap doesn't weigh much. Plus, my legs would get super strong and I figured that it might help attract the ladies!

Raghav, a fair boy with average physique, simple parted hair and a very honest disposition, emerged from the bathroom for the first time, he declared, "Hey, guys, this bathroom is too tiny. I can't live like this. Our other roommate, Kabeer, the ever sarcastic, insult-slinging jokester replied, "Do you like to take a morning stroll around the bathroom while you pee?"

Raghav, who did not pick up on the subtleties of sarcasm and rarely, if ever, knew when he was being made fun of, stood there stone-faced and replied, "There's no bath."

"Bath? What are you, four?"

"No, I am nineteen."

Looking around the room, as if he had an audience of a hundred, Kabeer continued without missing a beat. "Baby Raghav needs his bath, folks. Bring in the Epsom salts and the rubber ducky." At Raghav's blank stare, Kabeer decided to drop the joke and simply said, "That's what deodorant is for."

Kabeer Bastawala had a tanned complexion with naturally spiky hair. His speech included a lot of slang, definitions for which may never be found, even in a dictionary of slangs. Getting drunk, gambling and indulging in pornography were his daily "assignments." He never combed his hair, almost never bathed, and always ironed his clothes in place of washing them. If ever he smelled good (for a change) we would tease him.

"Kabeer, you only waited three days to take a shower? That's like a record for you."

"Your memory sucks, jerk," he'd say, "it's been *five* days!"

Kabeer could sure dish out insults on anyone. In fact some people were hesitant and even scared, to be around him and his "killing mockery."

We named our apartment *Bangla* no. 410, which soon became infamous for our loud music and late-night shenanigans. I can't count the number of times a night-shift cop knocked on our door, having been summoned by our irate neighbors to tell us to shut the hell up.

We had a room on the eastern side of the apartment. From the window, we could see the city. It stayed peaceful and quiet only when we were not there. Kabeer invested in some binoculars, which we tied to our window in the hopes that no beautiful woman passing by would escape our spying eyes.

Our room was full of what we will call a 'fragrance,' for lack of a more disgusting term, as we may have washed our bed sheets four times in the four years we resided there. We often found lizards and cockroaches in our bathroom, but we didn't blink an eyelid. It was part of the college lifestyle.

The most 'sophisticated' spot in our bedroom was the desk that we kept between our beds. Due to the morning rush to get ready for class, our entire wardrobe would end up piling up on our beds, and spilling over onto the desk. While going to bed, I would simply clear off a space just big enough to fit myself in. In addition to the lizards and cockroaches, seasonal mosquitoes used to rain down on us at night and almost eat us alive while sleeping.

Raghav, who became Raghu for us in a short span, was an interesting fellow as well, but in a -very different way from Kabeer. No matter what happened, he would always see the silver lining. This, of course, would annoy the hell out of Kabeer. I adored Raghu's sweet simplicity, but I never passed on a chance to laugh at his expense when Kabeer teased him. Anyway, he was honest and trustworthy. Had I had million dollars as cash in a locker, I would probably handover the keys to him rather than keeping them for myself.

So, that's us – the three people who inhabited at *Bangla* 410 – Kabeer, Raghu and I. Our apartment was fully furnished for the student-bachelor lifestyle, posters on the walls, kitchen-turned storage room, 'cause we never cooked and of course the beer cooler a.k. a our refrigerator.

One day I was futzing around in our small sitting room when I saw Raghu frantically writing something.

"Hey Raghu, what are you doing?" I asked. Kabeer emerged from his room and jumped in.

"Are you writing a love letter?" He joked.

"No, buddy. I'm doing tomorrow's assignment," he replied, sounding tensed.

"Ha! He is doing the assignment all by himself. Fake engineer!" Kabeer replied.

We never did homework on our own. We were all engineering majors and we helped each other with our assignments, if we did them at all.

Our routine was relatively hectic, as going to classes ate up most of the day. The college was located an hour away from *Bangla* 410, and if you missed the bus you were better off staying home as it took hours for another bus to arrive. Classes were scheduled with only a grace period of ten minutes in between. Trudging from one lecture to another became more and more tedious as the day wore on. Studying to become an engineer was dull and mind-numbing, as it was stemming less from the desire of many, and more from familial expectation and unspoken societal formality. Not so strangely, this made us proud no matter what actually we learn in the classroom! In fact, sitting at the food court was far more productive and happening. Not only would we use the time to complete assignments, an obvious source of knowledge, we also shared stories – gossiping and mimicking classmates and professors – which entertained us considerably. Last but not least, were the delicious, possibly mind-altering *chai* and *samosas*.

Out of four years of Engineering, two years go in finishing assignments; the period which is time-consuming and futile. Why, you ask? Well, because… CTRL+C, CTRL+V (*if you know what I mean*). There were sixty students per class and if the professor checked each assignment with the care necessary to catch the lethargy with which we approached an assignment, they wouldn't turn in our grades until we were old and gray. Exams were the cruelest part of our engineering studies. If you asked any engineering student what his biggest exam-day dream was, the most common answer would be to get thirty-five out of hundred. That was the university's minimum passing score.

As a *baniya* – an occupational caste made up of ancestral retail business owners, bankers and money lenders – I had always seen myself saving money and taking care of the ancestral business, but my dad's retail shop was old-fashioned. I had dreams of starting a business of my own, but I always had people around me who encouraged me to study engineering. It seemed to have become the modern day equivalent of the ancestral business and no one ever enlightened me of any other career options. My only aim was to study enough to get that bare minimum. If you were one of those rare people who wanted to score higher in your exams, you simply wrote more pages. Quantity over quality was the key.

2

HEARTBEATS OF ENGINEERING

After missing the bus too many times, I decided to invest in an alternate mode of transportation. I bought a used red *Pulsar* motorcycle with orange and white flame-like designs on it. I loved that bike. For four years, she was my constant companion. There was only one small problem: she was a voracious petrol-guzzler, never good news for my wallet. I don't remember servicing the bike once through all four years.

One day, the aforementioned core group planned to go out for movie together. We reached the theatre and stood in line for tickets. I was getting bored of the conversation when I looked over and saw Sonia; the long-lost, prettier-than-ever Sonia.

She and I went to the same grade school but we didn't run in the same circles back then. She was the ultra-studious sort, whereas I was flirtatious and goofy and didn't care much about my grades in school. I took a deep breath and pushed my way through the mob of movie-goers. She was surprised to see me and I couldn't tell if that was a good thing or not. She had come with her best friend, Meenal, whom I had also known back during school days. I stood there and chatted with them, trying to gauge what my chances would be: *you know what I mean*. The movie had already started. We entered the hall in a hurry and I apologized profusely for delaying us. The subtext of my apology was, "My perpetual hunt for a mate was probably coming to an end."

Sonia was always very pretty, which stands to reason, as she was *Punjabi*, Today she looked especially lovely as she glowed with the confidence and independence that you acquire upon moving out of your parents' shadow. She was pursuing a Chartered Accountant (CA) course in Indore, which seemed to be her goal. Her father was an accountant, hence his desire to see her succeed as a CA. She was a decent, fun-loving, extroverted individual who was sensitive about the littlest of things. After finishing the movie I asked for her phone number, which she gave with indifference.

No wonder, I started sending her texts that very night. I put words together carefully, making sure not to cross the thin line between friendship and flirting, though sometimes I did. She always replied, even if it was just a word or a smiley face. In fact, rarely did she respond with more than a couple words, and most of the time it just said, "That's funny." Funny? Well, hey, that's not a rejection! So, what took from that text was, "You're funny, go ahead and keep sending me more messages!"

Valentine's Day – or rather my festival – was just a week after we met. It was my tradition to send a flirtatious message to all the female contacts on my phone, saying my all-time favorite phrase, "Honey, I love you." Many of my close friends would reply, saying, "You're funny Kartik, I love you too!"

Those who didn't respond knew very well that it was my Valentine's Day tradition. And this year, by the grace of God, that list included Sonia. Without any hesitation, I hit send on the very same message, which read "Honey, I love you," and wondered how she would respond. Hoping, perhaps, that she might be glad to be loved by me on this crazy day of celebrating love.

Turns out I didn't have to wait long.

The whooshing proof that the message was sent had barely ended when my phone rang. She definitely sounded exasperated.

"What is this?" She did not give me time to answer. "Why did you send me this message?"

I put on a tone of jest in my voice, but I'm sure she could sense the fear under that air of jest. "I'm so sorry…I was just kidding!" I retorted, laughing nervously, trying to lighten the mood a bit. She wasn't buying it.

"We are just friends and I don't expect this kind of message from you. Goodnight." She hung up without letting me say another word, but I felt that act had ruffled feathers. I decided to give her a little space, and didn't text her the next day. I did, however, keep checking my phone to see if she'd had a change of heart, but the only message I got was a straggler from the day before. An old friend saying, "Dear Kartik. It wouldn't be Valentine's Day without your text message ☺" That made me smile, but I sure wished it had been Sonia who'd sent that message.

The next day I decided that if I hadn't heard from her by 6:00 PM I would send her another apology text and ask her to forgive me. And guess what? I had to do! After an hour, my phone rang. I answered it without even looking at the display. When I heard her voice, my heart jumped.

It took me two days to convince her. Finally, we met at *Shake & Bake*, a little café full of chocolates, cakes and teeny-boppers. I turned on my charm and tried to show her my romantic side.

"Sonia, that message really was just in jest. Umm…but, to be honest, I do have feelings for you. When I saw you at the theatre the other night, I couldn't believe my eyes. You are so beautiful, and I had such a crush on you since middle school, and I thought it must be fate that I was running into you again after all this time! Back then, I didn't have the guts to tell you, but now there is no point in hiding how I feel. Even if you don't feel the same way, I will never regret that I was able to be open and honest with you. Is it possible that you feel the same way?"

She seemed a little nervous after listening to my profession of love for her, and even seemed to cringe at the way I was expressing my thoughts and emotions.

"No, Kartik, it's not possible."

"Oh. Okay. Are you upset that I told you how I felt?" She seemed upset, but maybe she was just uncomfortable.

"I don't mind you expressing yourself," she replied, "but I don't want to give you any false hope by sugar-coating my answer. Please understand and stop thinking about me that way."

I couldn't believe how bluntly she'd refused my gentle proposal. I couldn't find the reason but I was upset.

In order to take my mind off the jarring rejection, I focused on the next round of exams. The easiest way to pass engineering exams was to refer a guide called the *Bhavani Publications*. They were like short notes; rather I would call it – *savior*, for students of engineering. Certainly familiarizing myself with sixty pages of *Bhavani* would be easier than trying to sift through and understand 300 pages of a boring, antiquated, and enormous textbook.

But that wasn't enough for Kabeer. It was the first year and we were extremely scared of the Basic Electrical Engineering (BEE) exam. Kabeer was usually involved in college politics and one common activity included buying question papers a day before the exam. And he would sell them too, if he had the chance.

Once, we bought the exam paper from his source to score high. Though Raghu was not in favor, he slipped in the end. We reached college confidently after preparing the answers to the questions. The campus was ablaze with students cramming information into their heads at the last minute. We looked at each other and simply started laughing at them. We entered the exam hall. Looking at the first question, my heart stopped. I glanced at the other questions and the world went silent. I looked at Raghu. His eyes appeared to be sinking in Onion sauce. He was hitting his head against his desk, mouthing the words *"fuck you!"* Only one question was the same from the exam paper we bought. ONE QUESTION! We both shot Kabeer a look of intense anger. He gave us all a guilty smile and chirped, "Guess we're all failing, bro." We left the hall within an hour, as we had absolutely nothing to write. After a week, we got our tests back. Marks were as follows out of 100: Raghu 23; me 18 and Kabeer 12.

Raghu, who had been a relatively-innocent bystander and against this idea all along, was extremely disappointed. We reminded him that he did better than any of us, but that didn't seem to raise his spirits in the slightest. He disappeared into his room and locked his door. That gave us our first taste of failure.

In the midst of buying exam question papers and skipping class to rub shoulders with others in the food court, I continued the chase for Sonia. It had been a month since her refusal to see me as anything but a friend, but that didn't stop me from expressing my feelings any chance I got, just in case she'd changed her mind. But a month, I felt, was long enough and I had reached my threshold. I sent her a text, asking her to meet one last time at *Shake & Bake* at 5 PM. I got her a small bouquet and a heart-shaped card from Rahul's Gift Shop that was opposite *Shake & Bake*. My plan was to impress her with this charming and romantic gesture, and if she didn't say yes this time, I would abandon this futile chase and move on. I tucked the flowers under the table and put the card under my leg. I glanced at my watch. 4:59 PM. The bell on the door of the café rung quite a few times and every time I looked up I was disappointed, until she arrived.

Sonia looked beautiful. She wore a low-necked black tank top with a long purple skirt that swirled breezily as she walked. As she sat down, we smiled at each other. Her smile was a bit tense but I hoped that would change. I stayed silent and just looked into her eyes, smiling. At first, it seemed, she couldn't help but smile back. But then she began to shift uncomfortably. She didn't seem to be sure of what I was up to, and when she asked, I simply shrugged, smiled and looked into her eyes. After a few minutes, she gave up and said, "This was obviously a waste of time. If you really don't have anything to say, I'm leaving." She stood up and reached for her purse, which she had slung over the back of her chair.

"Wait!" I blurted out, before I could think twice. I took a deep breath and wanted to say something, anything, to make her stay, but I couldn't find words in that moment. I gestured to her to hold on. I reached for the flowers I'd hidden under the table. I stood up and held the flowers out to her. She took a step towards the table and accepted the flowers, smelling them before placing them on the table and sitting down again.

"Thanks, Kartik. They're beautiful, but what's this all about? What's with the silent treatment and then the peace offering? I don't get it."

"Sonia," I began, "I never…I didn't *decide* to like you but…it just…It happened. And I know I came on a little strong right from the start, but that's only because something changed in me the night I saw you at the movies. I've never felt this way about anyone and it scares the hell out of me. I really like you and I feel like this is just…right, you know? I feel like we're supposed to be together — at least for now — but if you think I'm wrong tell me and I'll stop." I swallowed hard as I waited for her to say something. In my head, I gave myself a nice big pat on the back. I didn't plan to say any of that! It just came out, and the best part was that I meant every word of it. Sonia looked down, unable to make eye contact with me. Her silence was starting to worry me. I sat in the discomfort of that silence for a moment, and then I nudged the flowers gently towards her and said, "I'm sorry I bothered you. Enjoy the flowers."

In that last month, I had learned enough about Sonia to know that if I got up to leave, she would stop me. And that's exactly what happened. I sat down slowly and waited for her to say what was on her mind. I figured I owed her the silence. After a moment, she took my hand, sighed deeply, and said, "Kartik, I…I like you too, but…"

"But what?" I asked softly. "I was afraid." She almost whispered those words.

"You *were* afraid?" I asked.

"Yes."

"Of me?" I said in a goofy tone but she laughed and said, "More like a relationship in general." She said volumes with her eyes that said something from her past made her afraid.

"And now?" I tried to hold back my excitement. A sweet, adorable smile spread across her face, and she said, "I am less afraid with you."

I jumped out of my chair and started dancing. I couldn't contain myself! I was so happy. She just laughed and took my hand and pulled me back into my seat and we shared a moment of confort, knowing silence.

We enjoyed the moment until my cell phone rang and a stoic photo of my father appeared, which broke the silence and the mood.

3

HAPPINESS IS VISITING HOME

When you live away from home, visiting family, and meeting friends and relatives in your hometown is a luxury. My hometown was Ratlam, a town in Madhya Pradesh in Central India, which was known for the creation of *Ratlami Sev*, a delicious deep-fried snack made with chickpea flour, herbs, and spices. Scrumptious! Ratlam was a typical town of around two lakh population that flourished based on relationships unlike in metropolitan cities, which grow based on commerce and technology. Those of us born and raised there, knew everyone.

Another thing about these towns is that they never change; from the people standing at the *paan* shops to the dogs roaming on the streets. I tried to visit Ratlam once every few months. I couldn't go much longer than that without getting a fix of my mom's cooking.

It wasn't a long walk from the station, but with a heavy backpack, it felt like I was walking for an eternity. I strolled along, taking in the familiar sights and sounds. I was just so eager to be back home! After a few more agonizing minutes of walking, I finally turned into my street. This was the street I grew up on, where I spent my childhood, my awkward teenage years, and where I transitioned into a young adult. It wasn't just my house, but the entire street felt like home.

As soon as I entered my house, I saw my mother get up from the sofa, looking as though she had been lingering there for hours, awaiting my arrival. Her shadow flickered with excitement, then faded as she, herself, emerged with her arms wide, saying, "My son! My son has come home!" I dropped my backpack ran up to hug her. It was a quick, tight embrace, followed by the question that had obviously been on her mind for the entire duration that she waited, "What would you like to eat?" She listed all the dishes she had spent the last two days making for me. I made a beeline to the kitchen, my favorite place in the entire house. Seeing the array of delicious dishes, I just couldn't control myself. I started picking at the food directly from the casserole. My mother immediately brought out a plate and served some of the choicest of the delicacies and sat me down at the table. She stood there, watching me. The more I ate, the happier she became. "Sit down!" I said, "You're making me nervous."

Just then, my little monster of a younger sister came sauntering in. Out of sheer habit, I threw my arms around my plate and shielded it with my body. She was known for snatching food off my plate. Aditi, my adorable little sister, was three years younger and three times feistier than me. She was rather spoilt, and would throw a full-blown tantrum if she didn't get her way. She brought out the stubbornness in me. "What'd you bring me?" Aditi asked, looking at my plate and planning her strategy.

"Nothing, runt!" I said, and sat up straight, revealing the plate, as if silently challenging her to a duel.

"If you haven't gotten me anything, go back to Indore. Junk you are!" She lunged for my plate, stealthily bringing up one hand in defense while using the other to snatch a samosa. I expected this move, so I returned the favor by grabbing her hand and kicking her shin under the table. She yelped and dropped the samosa. She shot me a sly smile, took one last look at my plate, and disappeared into the shadows with a slight limp. It was a fun part of my family's dynamic. There are always two sides to a coin. If playful rivalry with my sister was one side of it, absolute fear of our father was the other.

My father was a very religious man. He would put a holy mark called the *tilak* on his forehead, even while he slept, which was not a common practice. He was quite a harsh disciplinarian with an authoritative disposition and militaristic approach to cleanliness. He used to take one look at me and say in his deep, intimidating voice, "How you will survive the rest of your life, only God knows!" He wanted his children to be successful. But, we just wanted to be accepted and loved for who we were. Instead, we always wondered what was wrong with us.

After my snack, I retreated to my room to unpack and rest for a bit. I opened my eyes and saw that the sun had set and the evening was on us. My father was likely to return home any time now. Out of sheer habit, I got up and straightened the bed. I pulled the sheets so tight that there was no evidence anyone had been there in months. I went downstairs to find my sister habitually making the same preparations for our father's return in her room.

She switched channels from MTV to one of the news channels. She spotted me snooping at the bottom of the stairs.

"You wanna help me out here?"

When my father was involved, I didn't argue. But I did shoot her a sarcastic look, letting her know that we would continue our feud later.

She carried leftover food to the kitchen while I straightened out the living room, erasing all evidence of life inside the house. We lived in constant fear that he might punish us for our unconscious mistakes. It was almost like we weren't allowed to be human.

He entered the house saying, *"Hare Krishna!"* as he always did, for he was an ardent devotee of Lord Krishna. We lined up at the door to greet him, as was our daily routine. His dutiful little army, awaiting his orders. He seemed happy, as happy as a man like he could be, to see me home. I expected him to ask "How was your journey?" Or say, "I see you made it safely." Or perhaps, "You are looking well, son, thanks for making the trip to visit your dear old dad."

Instead, his bold voice rang out in the only way he knew how to connect – with a demand. "Kartik get me a glass of water." I tried to convince myself that it was his way of welcoming me home, his way of feeling close to me. In that moment, though, I felt like I had not even gone to Indore.

We had a good conversation that evening, and by conversation I usually mean lecture. It was just his way – he would speak far more than he would listen. That night, however it was more like an interview, and it was the closest we'd ever come to having a casual chit-chat.

With his first sip of tea, he asked, "So, how are your studies going?"

"Good." I said with a shrug.

He put the cup down, and in his deepest, sternest voice, he said, "Work as hard as you can. It is the key to success." I never understood (or perhaps simply didn't agree with) this philosophy. But it was easier to let him think that I was on his side. "Yeah!" I said, shrugging internally.

Satisfied, he picked up the cup of tea again. With the second sip came the second question, "Are you eating well?"

Proudly, I began to list the many traditional Indian foods that had become staples in my daily diet. I started with breakfast. As I began talking about my lunch regimen, my father grumbled, saying, "What nonsense do you eat? Eat something healthy like fruit, almonds and cashews. Drink milk, as this will…"

With a nod, he took his third sip and asked about my friends. What he was really asking was about the friends who get higher marks. I told him about my roommates and how we helped each other with our studies. He didn't need to know about the kind of mischief we got ourselves mixed up with. In fact, he would've locked me up in a basement and never let me see the light of day if he'd known what really went on in that apartment.

He placed his cup down. This must be serious. "Do you go to the temple?" His voice was heavy, as if he suspected me of foul play.

Instantly I thought of *Shake & Bake*. That had certainly been a sort of temple for me, so I felt justified in saying, "Yes…sometimes!"

He was glad to hear this. "Do you do *Yoga* and *Pranayam?*" I was stuck on this one or I risked being caught in the lie. To me, these questions were trivial and, to an extent, torturous. I racked my brain for something in my life that was comparable to *Yoga* and *Pranayam* – a practice of conscious, steady breathing which help making the mind calm and focused – but in truth, I had never been in the habit of such a practice, even while living at home. He waited for my answer. My mind, of course, went to Sonia. I happily thought of picking her up in the morning and surprising her at her bus stop…She sparked my synapses, but stilled my mind. She was my *Pranayam.* "Yes, but mostly on weekends."

"Good!" he said, instantly, as if his very life depended on that answer. "Try to do it every day. It's good for your health. Especially for your mind…you most certainly need it for concentration!" I looked at him with a curious face. "You tend to forget things quickly!" I just smiled and nodded. Letting him believe that he was having a profound effect on how I'd live my life was a good thing.

"What do you do in the evenings, and on weekends?" This was the biggest question of all. I knew what he was really trying to convey was, "Don't fuck around and waste my hard-earned money!" I wasn't about to tell him what really went on in my world – that was a secret truly worth keeping – so I kept it simple and to the point.

"Nothing much. A few of my friends and I may go out for dinner on the weekends, but the rest of the time

I do homework, study for exams, write papers. The usual college stuff."

These discussions were like football games. I was constantly on the defensive, playing with caution and precision, and tracking moves of every player. It was exhausting.

Apparently pleased with my answers, he began discussing some of his philosophies of life. I tuned out, going over our interview in my head, trying to track every detail so I wouldn't be caught lying if there was ever a question on any of it again. The next thing I heard was his booming, authoritative voice telling us to go to bed. I glanced up at the clock and saw that it was still relatively early. At my apartment, I wouldn't have even eaten dinner by this time. But my father, being a "man of principles," expected us to adhere to the age-old saying: *Early to bed, early to rise.* College life had certainly changed that! My new saying went something like this: *Late to lectures, up late tonight.* Once again, I made him believe that I would follow his orders, but had no intention of going to bed any time soon.

Among other things, I had to call Sonia and, in the words of my father, "God only knows" how long that phone call would last. And last it did. We talked for hours that night, and every night that I was away. The routine continued for a month till Indore called me to start the next chapter of life.

4

~

THE MBA BUG STRIKES BACK

When I got back to Indore a week later, as I came out of the station, I was surprised to find Sonia waiting for me with a beautiful bouquet. It was very similar to the one I had given her the night I tested out my silence theory and almost lost her for good. I don't even know if she noticed, but I enjoyed the inside joke.

I gave her a warm hug and accepted the flowers with a chuckle and a big smile. "I'm starving!" she said, with a playful nudge. I waited for you. I hope you're hungry too."

"Famished!" I lied. Of course my mother overfed me before I left, but I knew that by the time we would sit down and assumed that my appetite would have surely returned. We ate a brunch fit for kings. I watched her lips as she spoke about who-knows-what, and I suddenly felt this surge of emotion.

"I love you," I blurted. She stopped mid-sentence – I think she was expressing how excited she was about school starting again – and stared at me for what felt like eons. I was just about to take it all back and apologize for saying something so stupid, when a smile spread across her face. I saw the tears welling up in her eyes. Yep…This was love!

With the completion of exactly half of my journey into the course, I began my third year, braced with the knowledge that I could complete (and pass) my exams without having to do much work. My half-assed approach to my studies allowed me plenty of time to get distracted with thoughts of what I would do after obtaining this unwanted degree. I wasn't satisfied with my achievements thus far, and I started obsessing about what *would* satisfy me. Gaining admission into this average engineering college gradually made me feel quite below-average. I was bored and I needed to figure out what would ignite the inspiration that festered beneath this thick layer of discontentment.

I didn't really care about good grades or excellent test scores. I was a dreamer, and I believed I could reach extraordinary heights if I dreamed big enough. "On a wing and a prayer," Sonia would say. This phrase had its bad connotations, but I took it as a good thing. Staying in touch with my younger, dreamier self would help me achieve greatness as an entrepreneur. Good grades are for suckers content with mediocrity. The entrepreneurial route seemed more glamorous, but I had no idea what my business would consist of. Would I sell products? services? dreams? It remained to be seen. I couldn't concentrate on the details when I was attending eight hours of technical lectures a week, mired in assignments and constant exam pressure. Business was my passion and learning management skills was the necessity. The MBA Bug ran in my nerves.

A degree, not typically from India this time, but the USA! I didn't know why I thought of only the USA but it was the way it was. If I did that, the world would be my oyster.

One day, Kabeer, Raghu and I were chatting in the hall. Out of the blue, Raghu changed the trajectory of the conversation into something profound.

"Guys, I have a crisis here. I mean, there are these two potential paths: what society wants us to do, and what we want to do. What should be the priority?"

"The third option: beer and cigarettes, and girls." Kabeer chuckled.

Raghu looked at me. I shrugged and said, "I'm with Kabeer on this one!"

"I'm serious, guys!" Raghu said. We knew he was serious, and that's why we joked about it. I think it made us collectively uncomfortable to talk about such heavy things. Our dynamic included crass jokes, small talk, and bashing our boring teachers. This was new territory.

"Are you gonna start dumping your philosophy on life and career on us?" Kabeer asked sarcastically. Beneath it was a tinge of fear.

"Yes. That's what friends are for. We have to do something after graduating, right?" We could see that Raghu wasn't going to let this go. Perhaps that was a good thing.

Kabeer said, "Okay, so…What are you gonna do?"

"Well, of course I'd like to get into one of the top companies, you know, the ones known for their reputation and credibility. But if they don't accept me, I might just do a Masters in Technology," Raghu explained.

"Masters of Technology?" Kabeer exclaimed. "Ach! Why?"

Raghu's tone took on a more defensive edge. "Because there's less competition. And if nothing happens after M.Tech, I could always get a job lecturing at of those new engineering college that pop up everywhere." We laughed. It's funny because it's true. I noticed that Kabeer wasn't laughing.

"Wow, you don't think very highly of yourself!" Kabeer said. He began mocking him, exaggerating his voice and body language. "I want to go to a fancy school and get a fancy degree, but they probably won't let me in, so I'll just do what every other shmuck does, and be miserable for the rest of my life."

Raghu shot him a disapproving glare. "First of all, I do not move my hands like that when I speak. Second, I'm just being realistic. It doesn't hurt to have a back-up plan."

After a continued sincere conversation by Raghu, Kabeer shared, "My parents are unlike all other parents," Kabeer said. "They don't expect me to go into any field in particular. They simply tell me to do whatever I like. But that's where I get stuck. It scares me because I guess I really don't know what I like." Wow. This really was the deepest and most serious discussion we'd ever had. Of course, someone had to bring it back to the lighter side of things.

Mustering his most serious expression, Raghu said, "Then you'd better open a cigarette shop! You know, you like cigarettes!" He broke his sarcastically serious expression and gave me a playful punch on the shoulder.

I gave him my back, "C'mon, no way! He would smoke it all, and there'd be nothing left for the customers. Not a great business model."

"What do *you* know about business models?" Raghu asked, getting in on the banter.

"Not a whole lot," I admitted. "That's why I want to get a degree in it – an MBA!"

"What's that? A Master of *Baniya* Administration?" Raghu retorted, and they burst into laughter.

Through the laughter, Kabeer joked, "He's gonna get an MBA in RSM." He started laughing even harder, but none of us knew what the hell that meant.

"What is RSM?" I asked.

"Ratlami Sev Manufacturing." They erupted into laughter "Hahaha…laugh all you want. You'll laugh me all the way to the US." The laughter stopped and they all stared at me, "And from where do you want to do your RSM course?" They were not letting go.

I tried to be defensive and strong, "USA!"

Kabeer fell from the bed laughing and choking.

"Go wash your ass first. USA!"

"Baby, come to the washroom," Raghu added more salt.

They started chanting, "MBA in the US. MBA in the US."

"Shut up, assholes!" I said, but I had to yell to be heard over their obnoxiousness.

Raghu motioned for him to stop and he obliged. "Okay, okay…But why the USA?" asked Raghu sincerely.

"Isn't that obvious? To have an awesome life and to earn in dollars!" They grumbled and nodded. It should've been obvious. "And to escape the excruciating competition to get into IIM. Which, for me, would be like hitting my head against a wall repeatedly." I took a deep breath and continued. "Plus, just imagine how fashionable it would be to work in the US! People back home would say, "Oh wow, he works in Manhattan? Amazing!" Kabeer looked down, held his head in his hand and said, "Will somebody please wake him up?"

"On it!" Raghu said. "That is a terrible idea! Do you know how expensive that would be? Not to mention your terrible track record and below-average grades! What makes you think you'll get into a University there? You're dreaming." Kabeer looked at Raghu as if he hadn't expected him to go that far. Maybe he could have playfully slapped me to wake me up, or perhaps given me a laundry list of reasons to stay in India: Sonia, my family, my friends, tradition, convention, or any number of other reasons. But no, he went for the jugular.

I held my breath for a moment, unsure of how to react. Finally, I smiled and said: "You know what? I love my dad a little more now. Thanks for the pep-talk."

And that was the end of that.

5

LAST CAMPUS – ANY SURPRISE?

It was our final year of engineering, and the season for IT companies to collect their raw materials from all the B.E. factories had started. Metaphorically, of course! All these 'factories' i.e. colleges would transport their 'eligible products' i.e. students who'd maintained 60% marks or higher in B.E. to the common 'warehouse' i.e. open campus.

In preparation for this season, we had to take a series of tests so that each recruiting company had a tangible record of our knowledge and skills. One company, Infotys Solutions, was highly coveted. I took that exam with a do-or-die attitude. Being selected by this company meant being guaranteed a good job with a reputable company right out of school.

After the exam, they announced the results. With every name being called, there were both, hope and distress. Once, they even said Kartik, and my heart jumped out of my chest as I began a little victory dance. But it was Kartik Sharma, not me, as the surname would reveal. I went from pure elation to catastrophic disappointment within a millisecond. I was so busy trying to get my heartbeat to return to normal, I almost missed it when a familiar name was called.

"Raghav Nagar."

"What?" I said, snapping out of my reverie. Out of the corner of my eye, I saw Raghu drop to his knees, which confirmed that I had heard right. I wasn't sure whether to congratulate him, or concentrate on the remaining list, so I let him have his moment on his knees. There'd be plenty of time for celebration.

Finally, the announcer said; "That's it! Congratulations to those of you who were selected. To those of you who were not, I wish you better luck next time."

It felt like the sky had fallen on me. Disappointment like I had never felt before washed over me. Even knowing that engineering was not my passion, that I would go on to do much more interesting things with my life, I was still hurt. I had let myself down. It was a definite blow to my ego. As the crowd dispersed, I noticed people celebrating their friends' selections, all in a half-hearted way. It was difficult in that moment to be happy for someone who got something you wanted. Even if you didn't really want it. We all gave Raghu half-hearted pats on the back and congratulated him with just as much energy as we could muster and then returned to *Bangla* no. 410 in silence.

Just before we reached home, Raghu looked at the two of us and said with a smile, "Guys, are you really that disappointed?"

"No, we are born with sad faces," Kabeer said with biting sarcasm.

"But…why?"

We looked at each other, not really understanding the question. We all wanted to hear our names being called. We all wanted to be selected.

"Dosto!" He said. Look, happiness does not come from a company that you care nothing about. Happiness is walking your own path. Kartik wants to get his MBA. This wasn't an admissions exam! Kabeer doesn't know what he wants to do. There's no reason to get upset about missing a target you never aimed to achieve in the first place."

"Salute! Salute! Salute! He is our new lecturer!" Kabeer joked defensively. But in all honesty, Raghu was right. We walked away from that conversation feeling a little lighter. The bruise to our egos would heal, and perhaps we would focus on the things that really mattered to us.

Still, after more and more companies made their decisions on whom they had selected, and after failing to hear my name called each time, my confidence was at its lowest. I just kept telling myself, after each failure, that *it wasn't the end of the world.* In fact, it made me more inclined to get that MBA. *That* I would work hard for. *That* would pull me out of my discontentment.

Before the end of the final semester we had a long weekend. I decided to take the opportunity to go home, as it had been almost four months since I visited them last. When I arrived, it was evening – and a rather dark evening at that. By 'dark evening' I mean they cut the power from 6 PM to 8 PM in Ratlam. I found my way from the train station with only the glow of my cell phone.

The scene inside the house was the same as usual. My mom was trying to shove food down my throat. Fights with my sister Aditi were never-ending and this went on until my father walked in through the door. We didn't do our usual preparations for his arrival, but thankfully the drawing room was already clean and the television was off. The only thing we had to do was shut our mouths.

After dinner, the four of us sat in the drawing room. I steeled myself for the defending match that I was about to play. My dad, ever the tough man, sat stoically and waited for me to make eye contact before he shot off his first question. It was a new set of questions with the same goal: to make sure that I was keeping up with my studies and living the life he wanted me to live.

"How is life, Kartik? What is going on currently?" he asked casually, grabbing the newspaper.

"Everything is fine," I said, knowing my answer was broad.

"How's your semester coming along? You're in the seventh semester, now, right?" he asked.

"Dad I am in the eighth semester now." Was he testing me? Or did he really not know?

"Oh yes, I remember. How's your campus drive so far?"

Reluctantly I said, "Nothing positive…" And then as an afterthought, I added a positive spin. "… yet!"

"It's no wonder. Look at yourself! You stay up late, sleep in late, eat junk food all day, and don't maintain cleanliness. How do you expect to get selected?"

None of those reasons had anything to do with the selection process. I just sat there and listened to him as he continued to berate me and my habits, until he finally ended his tirade with his favorite philosophy: "Keep working hard. You know the key to success is hard work."

I nodded, as I always did, even though I didn't agree. This time, I decided to voice my mind. After a long pause, I said softly, "Dad I know hard work is important, but I think it is also important to know in which direction to focus that hard work."

He looked at me, dumbfounded. I smiled. I had never rendered my father speechless before this. I could see his wheels turning. I basked in the glory of my accomplishment because I had clearly struck a chord of some kind. I made my father think about things in a way that was foreign to him. I could see he wanted to say something, but wasn't quite sure where to begin.

"Look at the newspaper," he said, finally. "I see the photographs of toppers on the front page every day. Some of these students have to study under street lights, and still they pass their exams."

What did studying under a street light have to do with direction? What did toppers have to do with my stupid degree in engineering? Toppers, by the way, are what we call students who rank high in Arts-Science-Commerce-Board Exams, at school level. That's completely different from exams at college. I didn't expect him to understand, though. His generation was stuck in its ways. And being a businessman, he knew only his business. To him, everything was cut and dry. He didn't understand the intricacies of life for someone in the younger generation.

"How many companies are left to conduct interviews on your campus?" he asked.

"Three or four," I said, and tried to hide the eye-roll that accompanied my answer.

"Do you think you would clear any?"

"I will try, but…"

"But what?"

"I want to do my MBA," I said instantly. I just couldn't help myself – the words just fell out of my mouth. "I'm not really interested in being selected by any of these companies." My heart started racing. I had never let my dad see this side of me. I felt rebellious and powerful, but I tried to keep myself soft and meek on the outside so that I didn't lose traction.

"MBA. Yes, yes…what do you call it? The CAT?" He knew the name of the exam. That was impressive. Was the generation gap closing? "Will you go to IIM?" The fact that he wasn't shutting the idea down on the spot filled me with hope. I got a surge confidence and felt a sort of bravery I'd never experienced around my father. I decided to drop the bomb.

"No, I want to get my MBA in Manhattan."

"Where is that?"

"New York. USA."

"WHAT?" From his expression, I couldn't figure out whether he was shocked, surprised or angry. I took a deep breath and said it again, loud and clear this time. "I want to get my MBA in the USA. I believe that's where one can get the best education, and the greatest opportunities."

"How much will it cost?" It seemed a fitting question.

"I don't know. It's just a thought now. I have to do my research and figure it out."

My father was notably pensive for a moment. I could tell he wasn't ruling out the idea entirely, but he wasn't giving it the thumbs-up either. My dad had always lived in Ratlam. The biggest city he visited was Indore, and sending his child to the USA seemed unattainable and impractical to him. "I would say that it's best to focus on campus selections, first," he said. With that, he excused himself and told us all that we should go to bed.

The next afternoon, I sat with my mother on the balcony, sipping *chai* and making small talk. Breaking one of our many silences, she said, in a low voice, "Kartik, please don't go abroad. I don't care about a degree or money. I am happier with you being close to me!"

I never quite understood this sentiment. In my mind, there was nothing more important for a young man than to have a graduate degree from a university abroad. She would rather that I forego higher education and my happiness, because my absence would be too hard on her. Still, I didn't want her to be upset.

"Ma, I don't know for sure that I'm going anywhere. It's just a thought!" I knew I was determined to get my MBA in the USA, but there was no use in letting her fret about it until the plans were final. I knew deep down she would support me in any decision I would make.

6

I'M SORRY, HOW MUCH WILL IT COST?

The next morning, I returned to Indore. Sonia met me at the station, and in my excitement, I told her about my career plans. I told her how I stood up to my father, and he didn't shut down the idea, and that I could move ahead with my plans. I looked at her expectantly, hoping that she would burst out with excitement and give me a congratulatory hug and take me for a big feast to celebrate. On the contrary, she lowered her head and remained quiet.

"Aren't you excited for me?" I asked anxiously.

"I am, but…"

"But..?."

"What about us?" she asked, keeping her head down to avoid eye contact.

My heart skipped a beat. I hadn't even taken her into consideration. This idea had been flitting around the back of my mind for long, ever since I could remember. I was so wrapped up in my excitement for my future. It hadn't occurred to me how it might affect her. I didn't want her to know that she hadn't entered my mind during these discussions. It wasn't anything personal. I just hadn't thought that far ahead.

"Hey honey, it's just an initial thought. I don't know if it'll actually happen, and if it does, it's not for a lifetime! It's just a matter of year or two." That might have been a stretch, but I wanted it to seem like nothing. No time at all. I grabbed her and brought her close to me. "We are made for each other!" I squeezed her harder. "You know that, right?" She muttered a muffled "Uh-huh," with her face still buried in my chest. We lingered in our embrace for a moment longer. When she let go, she had a big smile on her face. I guess my words had lightened up the situation. She was ready to support my cause!

We talked about all the possible details and realizing that there was so much we didn't know, we decided to go to a counselor at college to get more information. I'd heard about Vinay Chaddha from The Global Institute, who was an expert on foreign education. Sonia helped me secure an appointment with him. She was amazing: making calls on my behalf, coming up with ideas to make this work, despite her wish deep down that I'd never leave. No matter how many times I was forced to turn her down for a movie date to focus on my plans, she remained my biggest cheerleader. I appreciated her more than ever. Her unconditional support meant the world to me.

On the day of the appointment, we entered Mr. Chaddha's office at The Global Institute. We were early. In front of us, there was a wall filled with photos of students in caps and gowns – students who were admitted to and had evidently graduated from one of the many foreign universities. A beautiful receptionist sat at a table under the poster, with a beaming smile.

"Please have a seat." She motioned to the high-backed chairs in the waiting area. "Mr. Chaddha will be with you shortly." We thanked her and sat down as instructed. The chairs made you sit up, like a boss would, in the posture that made anyone look important and tortured. I guess comfort doesn't get you in a college abroad. That was my interpretation of the situation, anyhow.

I couldn't help but look over at the wall of photos. I started imagining myself overseas, accepting my diploma after years of diligent study, a giant smile on my face, and a thumbs-up from my mom and dad who would be there to celebrate my victory. Suddenly, doubt came rushing in and destroyed my vision. Impossibility wielded its sword and began lashing out at hope. Just then, Sonia put a hand on my leg. Her warm, soothing touch calmed me instantly. I guess she'd seen the panic on my face.

Being from a middle class family had its advantages of studying and being close to home. Not only would it take great effort and dedication, it would also require a big fat bank account. Bigger and fatter than any bank account attached to any member of my family. I was doomed. I was in the middle of a bank-robbing fantasy when the receptionist asked us to go in.

We entered his office and saw that he was eating fruit salad.

"We're happy to wait if you'd like to finish your lunch." I said, thinking that it was quite rude to counsel someone with your mouth full and your attention elsewhere.

"No, no!" he said, swallowing and putting the plate aside. "Have a seat."

He appeared to be in his mid-forties with a fat tummy and thick, black-framed spectacles. As we took our seats, he reached over and snagged another fork-full of food from the plate and shoved it in his mouth.

Still chewing, he said, "Tell me…what can I do for you?"

I paused, wondering if I had made a mistake coming here. But he had such a good reputation and I was already there, sitting before him, so I figured I might as well get as much out of him as I could. "I am planning on getting an MBA from the US. Could you tell me what basic preparations are required?"

"You have to pass some exams, and then complete the application process for each school."

Ach! I knew that exams would be part of the equation. But the mere mention of the word gave me a headache. "What exams would I have to take?" I asked. He must have detected my hesitation.

"They're really not that difficult," he said, taking a slice of apple from his plate. "You just have to take the GMAT – for aptitude skills, and TOEFL – for English." And with that, the apple flew into his mouth. *Crunch, crunch, crunch.*

"How much time do you recommend one needs, to prepare for these exams?"

"It depends," *Crunch, crunch, crunch.* "I'd say the average is around three months."

That sounded like a short amount of time to me. I didn't want to sound too eager. I didn't want to get my hopes up. There was still the pressing question of costs.

"Sir, what would be the overall expense of the program…approximately?"

He adjusted his glasses, swallowed the last bit of the apple in his mouth and shrugged. "Twenty lakhs. That should be enough."

Are you fucking kidding me? That was Rs. 20,00,000. That was far more than my dad made in a year! I imagined him crying, which would never happen, of course, but if ever my dad would cry, it would be over money; money that he didn't have to send me to get my MBA in the US. Sonia and I exchanged a look. Impossible!

"What happened?" he asked politely.

I suddenly felt ashamed. In front of this beer-bellied, horn-rimmed, apple-chomping chump, I felt inferior because I couldn't afford to go to school overseas. "Umm… Nothing," I lied. "I guess I'll just have to check with my dad about the funds."

But Mr. Chaddha could see that wasn't all. He knew that checking with my dad would not yield the results I wanted. It must have been written all over my face. "Look," he said, leading us to the wall of photos within the walls of his own office. "Do you see these students smiling, in square caps and robes, holding their diplomas?" We nodded. "They all had the same doubts, starting out. But they made it. Do you know why?"

"Because they had money!" I said, with more of a defensive and dejected tone than I had anticipated.

"No. It was because they wanted it and they simply tried."

I stared at him, thinking that simply trying did not make twenty lakh rupees just show up at your doorstep. "Every journey starts with the first step. And what is the first step?"

Money! I wanted to say. But instead, I asked the question he wanted, to set him up for the punch line. "What is the first step?"

"The exams. If you manage to get decent scores, we will start the application process."

"We?" I asked. He explained that he would work with me every step of the way. He also explained that in America, there are payment plans and scholarships and ways to either get money or, at the very least, postpone payment of money to educational institutions. Sonia and I listened to him with awe. This man knew a lot. Despite his outwardly slob-like behavior, he seemed to have a good head for this stuff, and that's what I needed.

He recounted a few success stories from past clients of his, weaving in details of the lifestyle in the US and I couldn't help but imagine myself there. It could happen. It could!

"One more question.." I began. "What are the job prospects after completing an MBA? What is the basic salary one might get?"

"If you try hard and manage to get a decent job, the basic salary would be Rs. 2–2.5 lakh a month."

My eyes widened and Sonia and I shared another look. "Are you kidding me?" He shook his head, not realizing that my question was rhetorical. "That's almost the annual salary in IT on campus!" I could work with this. If I worked in the US for only a year after getting my MBA, I would be able to repay my entire loan.

"When do the classes start?" I asked.

"We have a new session starting next week."

I looked at Sonia. She gave me a smile. "Sign me up!" I said. For this I'd study hard. For this, I'd dedicate my precious time and energy. I left his office feeling lighter, more optimistic. My mind was conjuring up the future expecting global dreams to happen in reality.

7

THE ROBOTIC JUNGLE

It was the final month of the final year of the engineering course. One of my last hopes for my selection was ICOMP, an IT company based in Indore. Either my presumed intelligence was paying off, or the company was desperate: I was SELECTED! I turned to my friends and yelled, "Oh my gosh! I can't believe this!"

Excited about the job security, and still reeling from the ego boost at being the chosen one, I forgot all about taking the GMATs and prepared, instead, to join ICOMP. This was certainly a big achievement, but this is exactly what I *didn't* want.

After the training, I was placed with a project as a Java Developer. My world was confined to a cubicle with nothing but a desk, a chair, and a 17" computer screen. The stress levels were so high in that office that I could count on one hand the number of times I'd laughed, or shared a moment with my colleagues.

I had a dismal social life. In many ways, I felt like a robot: getting through the day emotionlessly, performing the tasks I was programmed to do. There was no camaraderie, and certainly no concept of appreciation. They were afraid that, should a manager compliment you for the work, you would demand a pay increase or, God forbid, a promotion.

But in five months, I decided that I was not cut out for the life of a doubt-ridden, fearful robot. I figured that the only way to escape this robotic jungle (aside from angling to get fired) was to apply for an MBA program. Just then, an image of that fat bespectacled man, Vinay Chaddha, popped into my head. I dug through my old papers, found his phone number, and gave him a call.

GMAT – EVERY JOURNEY BEGINS WITH THE FIRST STEP

I enrolled in GMAT classes (again). Only this time, I had five months of hell under my belt, and fire under my ass. I was going to ace this thing. Then, I found out that 'acing' was not quite the point. The best thing about GMAT, Vinay said, is that there was no percentile system. Which meant that the admissions were not rank-based, but profile-based. A profile was so much more than a score on a single test – which was very good news for me. Though it includes the GMAT score, it also takes into consideration experience, potential, personality and quality of application. Vinay Chaddha ensured that he'd help me build a strong profile.

The first day was a math class. I'd heard that the GMAT's math portion was relatively easy, but I had my doubts. Even after growing up with an accountant for a father, I never experienced ease with numbers and mathematical equations. I held my breath as the test sheets were handed out. I glared at the first question and exhaled as I read it. It was a greater-than/less-than equation. I re-read it to make sure I didn't misunderstand. It seemed almost too simple. I wrote the answer (greater than) and moved on. The next one was asked you to find the fifth angle of a pentagon. Remedial geometry. My eyes were filled with tears of joy. "I got this!" I thought. If this is as hard as it gets, I'll be in the US in no time! After class, some of the students were discussing how easy that was, and how this test was going to be a piece of cake. A small-framed boy who looked no older than twelve piped up in a pre-pubescent squeaky little voice, "Guys, guys…the math portion is easy! The difficult portion is going to be English." It was a warning that I didn't take seriously enough, until the next day.

Our second day, we had an English class. Confident from the previous day's triumph, I breathed easy. We were given a test sheet. The subject was reading comprehension and, as it turns out, I didn't comprehend a damn thing. Every multiple-choice option seemed like a possibility. I was confused, and didn't get a single answer right. My new goal was to improve my English skills. That night, I began digging into books on reading comprehension and vocabulary-building. I didn't touch a newspaper unless it was in English. While I was at it, I made it a point to watch only English programs on TV.

The second-biggest challenge was balancing this and my relationship with Sonia. Focused, for once in my life, on my studies, I wasn't left with much time to see her, to read her beautiful face and know what she was thinking or feeling. Our daily dates turned into weekly moments.

Shake & Bake started to miss us, I started to miss us, but there wasn't a damn thing I could do about it. Preparing for the GMAT was unforgiving. Study materials piled up like a football tackle gone wrong. I forever underestimated the amount of time I'd need to prepare for the next day's test sheet. I couldn't hide that fact. My bewildered state of mind started to bother Sonia more than I'd expected it would. The lesser time we spent together, the more possessive she got. She couldn't understand how I was choosing something else over her, never mind that it was to further my career and fulfill a dream of studying in the US.

Sonia didn't comprehend the immense pressure I was under to succeed at this. It meant a future for me. It may have even meant a future for us, but she didn't have that kind of vision at the moment. She seemed short-sighted and over-emotional.

THE BATTLE DAY

This was a nervous day, *not* because this was my first full-length computerized exam, *nor* because the result was going to be shown immediately following the exam, but because this was the most expensive exam I had ever taken. The exam fee was more than the combined total of every exam I'd ever taken.

The exam hall was bright with wall-to-wall plush carpeting, a beautifully painted ceiling, and about a myriad computers. Each test-taker was given their own, dedicated computer. As I plonked myself down, my heart raced with anticipation. As soon as I was done, I would know the results. I completed the exam with the concentration of a Chess player. The screen popped up in the end. "Do you want to see your results?" "Dude, what do you think

I'm doing here? OF COURSE I WANT TO SEE MY RESULTS!" I said in my mind.

My score flashed on the screen and I ran out of the hall the very next moment. I fumbled frantically for my cell phone. Vinay Chaddha – my inadvertent MBA mentor – had better answer his phone!

I had almost given up, but finally after the sixth ring, he picked up. "Hey Kartik, how did it go?"

"I give up," I wheezed.

"Why, what happened?" He was shocked. He knew how hard I'd studied, despite my breaks to appease Sonia. I was walking quickly, as far away from the testing facility as I could get.

"It was a disaster," I said, breathlessly. All that money I'd just wasted paying for that test! All that time I'd wasted studying and NOT being with Sonia! All for nothing! I felt like crying.

"Okay," his voice was sympathetic. The voice I wish my father would employ in such situations. "I want you to come to my office right away."

I entered his office with my head bowed low. He patted me on the back and his gentle, caring voice lulled me out of my depression. "Don't worry, you haven't lost the battle yet. As you know, your GMAT score is only a small part of the application. Your overall profile is still strong. Let's start the application process and see what comes up!" His pot-bellied perkiness was just enough to give me the hope I needed to proceed. That day I truly learned the importance of a motivating, high-spirited mentor.

LIFE GIVES YOU ONE CHANCE

I completed the application process for several universities, after extensive research and a whole lot of writing. This was an extremely expensive process…the price of each application was equivalent to the cost of a decent smart phone. And now, I just had to wait. A torturous, nail-biting couple of months were in store for me. Every day, I checked my inbox for an acceptance letter thinking that just one would do, and every day, my heart sank at the absence of such a letter. In the second month after I'd sent my applications, I went out of town for my cousin's wedding, and was unable to check my email for an entire week. It was a much-needed respite from the agony of waiting.

Upon my return, the first thing I did before even putting down my luggage was to open my inbox. My suitcase fell on the floor as my knees buckled. I stood frozen, glaring at the screen, disbelief filling every cell of my body. Today, I had made history. Today, against all odds, I received not one, but three acceptance letters! I wiped the screen of my computer – twice. I even pinched myself. I couldn't believe it. THREE!!! One was the University of Massachusetts, Boston. Boston! That was like a miniature New York. I could get down with that! When I was able to move again, I immediately called my new hero, Vinay Chaddha.

"I can't believe what has happened!" I said, feigning disappointment in my voice. He was silent for a second, mustering his courage to receive the bad news. "What has happened?" His voice was tense and I could feel the heaviness in his heart after all our hard work. I suddenly felt bad for the momentary deception, and immediately blurted: "Acceptance letters from *three universities!*"

I could hear the squeak in his voice as he jumped from his chair. "You did it! I am so happy for you…Congratulations! I need you to come to my office right away!" His happiness was akin to that of my own. He, too, had worked very hard to get my applications. I was excited to be the one to provide another photo for his reception wall.

When I reached, I scoped out a spot for my photo. I knew it would be awhile before graduation, but it was still very important. A moment later, he emerged and greeted me with an awkward high-five-turned-half-hug. We stepped into his office and sat in our usual spots across from each other.

"Congratulations again…you deserve it! One more vital step in this process, and then you'll be on your way to studying in the States."

"What step is that?" I thought that would be it. Get accepted, pack, and go to school. I forgot there was a whole ordeal around actually getting to The States.

"The visa interview," he said, as if it was no big deal. Taking my cue from him, I said, "I'll ace it. No problem." But suddenly, doubt bubbled up from my gut and, apparently, landed on my face. He detected it immediately, "What happened?"

"I've gotten this far and I'm really excited, but even if I ace the visa interview, I still won't be able to afford it. Everything's coming together except for the finances…the most important part of the whole plan."

"Don't worry. You just worry about preparing yourself for your first semester. I will work on the financial side of things."

I didn't quite know what he meant, but he seemed confident, so I took his word. Just one thing left to do! Baby New York, otherwise known as Boston, was only an interview away.

EVERY HAPPINESS DOESN'T BRING A SMILE

I take that back. *Two* things left to do: an interview and convincing Sonia and my family that I should go. I had to convince them that this was the best thing for me, and I had to, somehow, get them to support me in this decision. It was no small feat! I'd say the level of difficulty was astronomically higher than that of the GMAT. And you know how *well* I did on that…I took Sonia to *Shake & Bake*. We sat at our usual table and sipped our *chai* like it was any other day. After a few warming sips of tea, I mustered the courage to break the news. "I have something to tell you." I smiled lightly, not wanting to appear too excited before gauging her reaction.

"Okay," she blushed, which made me even more nervous. Was she expecting me to propose? I must've paused for an exceedingly long time, caught up in my thoughts when she said, "Please tell me now, Kartik. Please."

I took a deep breath. "I got accepted to three universities, Soni!" She was silent. I watched as the color drained from her face. She lowered her eyes and sarcastically shrugged her shoulders. "What's wrong?" I asked, already knowing the answer.

"Congratulations, Kartik! You will soon be in the States," she said, indifferently.

After a moment's silence, she continued, "I am happy for you but…did it ever occur to you that I might not want you to go? Do you even care about our relationship? I will be left alone here while you go gallivanting around the United States."

"I certainly won't be gallivanting," I said. "I will be studying hard and working, and missing you every moment. Soni, this success will be *ours.*"

"I don't want to be a hurdle but…will that success be worth being alone and miserable in the meantime?"

I reached across the table and lightly took her hand in mine. "It's only a matter of two years. Then we will be together again. Trust me."

She pulled her hand back. Not in anger, I don't think, just…in confusion. "I do trust you, but I'm scared. What if you love it there and never come back? What if you meet someone? "I don't want you to leave me," she almost whispered it as if it was the most difficult thing she'd ever said.

"Honey, I'm not leaving you. We will be in touch every day."

"What if I need you one day, and you're a million miles away?" I had no answer that would make the situation any easier. So I stayed silent. "I know your dreams are important," she continued. "But, honestly, you can achieve them here just as easily. What's the difference?"

"Honey, I'll make more in a month in the US than I will in an entire year in India. You remember what Vinay Chaddha said?"

"Karti, it is togetherness – not money – that makes us rich!"

There wasn't much I could say to that. We'd just have to agree. For her, having my arms around her was far more important than any degree, or the financial success. After a long, heated discussion, she gave up on words and her eyes filled with tears. I had no defense against tears. This wasn't a battle and feelings can never be conquered with logic, so I gave up on words, too, and simply held her in my arms.

THE ULTIMATE GREEN LIGHT

The day after my unsuccessful session with Sonia, I went home to discuss the situation with my family. The biggest hurdle was going to be getting the green light from my dad, especially with the exorbitant expenses involved with getting an MBA. This was a big step. The fees would not be in rupees, but in dollars. The only possible way was taking out a loan – something my father was never keen on doing.

"Tell me the whole situation," he seemed genuinely interested. He even turned off the TV and gave me his full attention.

"Dad, I got calls from three universities, the best of which is The University of Massachusetts, Boston."

"Is this University of *Mesaatuset*...how do you say it?"

"Massachusetts."

"Yeah, whatever it is...Is that in the top 10?" his all-time high expectation.

"Ummm...I don't know where it ranks, but it is a recognized university, and it's in Boston."

"Is that supposed to mean something to me?" he asked, the edge starting to return to his otherwise sincere tone.

"Boston is known for education. All the schools there are top-notch."

I could tell he wasn't convinced. Then came the big question. He put his glasses aside and scrunched his forehead and said, "How much will it cost?"

To avoid giving him a heart attack, I told him the discounted price. "It would be around twelve to eighteen lakhs."

I saw the smoke coming out of his ears. I had to think fast. "But I can apply for part-time jobs and scholarships." I held my breath, and watched as he processed all this information. His mind was racing, I could see it, but I didn't know which way it was going to go. Was he trying to think of ways to let me down easy, or was he scrolling through his bank accounts, seeing how feasible it would be to send me to Boston? After a few agonizing moments, he looked at my mom and said, "Let me check with the bank if we can get a student loan for you." I released my breath and did a little victory dance in my mind. I knew he had good standing and his bank would not deny him. My dreams were becoming a reality now.

"Kartik," my mother said, breaking her silence, "I will not let you out of India. I heard that once people go to the United States, they never return."

"Mom, I will return. I promise."

"I told you, you are not going anywhere. I don't want money; I don't want the kind of success that takes my child away."

I looked at my dad. *Help me out here!* He always wanted me to be a dashing success and it didn't matter where I lived, as long as I made him proud. He stayed silent, allowing my mother to express her woes without interruption. I tried to convince her that it would not be forever, but there was nothing I could say to change her mind. Her baby boy was not going anywhere. She was upset all day. Aditi, on the other hand, was excited to see me go. All she cared about was having gifts sent to her from the US. Little brat!

We didn't have a definite 'yes' from the bank yet, but it looked good and there was nothing more I could do from home, so I returned to Indore. Sonia met me at the station and before I could even say hello, she blurted, "Let's go to *Shake & Bake*. I want to discuss something with you."

Oh, man! Now what?! With both Sonia and my mother upset with me I felt the pit in my stomach expanding. Even if I do get the loan, and even if the visa interview goes well, I would still have two very strong and important women to contend with.

Sonia and I sat silently, and a little tense, for quite a while.

"Karti, I think you should go to the US," she paused and looked me right in the eyes. I could tell this wasn't easy for her to say. "You want to go, and I don't want to stop you." I instantly felt a ray of sensational happiness. "I don't want to hold you against your will. I don't want you to have regrets in the future. If you don't go because of me, that will only bring a gap between us." She took a deep breath and seemed to prepare herself for part two of this beautiful speech. "We can be together after two years, and you may never have this opportunity again. Move ahead, achieve your dreams. I will be here waiting for you, because I love you… and I always will."

I was so happy to hear her say that, but at the same time I felt guilty for wanting to leave, for wanting to achieve my dream of studying in the US. "Soni, I don't know what's going to happen. I do know one thing, though, it won't be easy living without you. It will be a struggle for both of us. I promise I will come back to you, because I love you, too. I don't care how challenging a long-distance relationship will be. I love you."

She smiled a little. I gave her a hug and said, "You know you are my best girlfriend."

She punched me lovingly on the arm, "I will kill you!" She said, and held me tight.

8

VISA INTERVIEW: A THIN LINE
BETWEEN RUPEE AND DOLLAR

I had never run this fast in my life. Had it been an Olympic sprint, I would have won the gold medal. I was running late…It was the day of the visa interview. With permission from both my father and my girlfriend, I went into the interview with confidence…With each word he wrote, my heart pounded harder, growing heavier with each beat. He looked up at me blankly… I couldn't tell from the guy's face if I was answering his questions to his liking, but after that excruciating pause, he said: **"Enjoy your stay in the States…Good Luck!"**

Oh My God, I did it…I did…I did it!

I couldn't believe what had happened. I felt tears of happiness well up in my eyes. I came out to the lobby, where Sonia was waiting for me. I was so grateful to her. I might have gone anyway, but having her blessing meant the world to me. I couldn't wait to share the news.

"I did it!" I said. It didn't come out as excited as I thought it would. To be honest, I wasn't sure how I felt about it. Part of me felt like celebrating – I just had my Visa approved! Part of me was sad at the prospect of leaving the love of my life behind. I could tell she had the same dichotomy of emotions happening for her. She gave me a short smile and then went silent. That silence was the scariest thing in the world at that moment. I looked in her eyes and lied outright, "Sonia, I still don't know what's going to happen." I was trying to make her and myself feel better. That was dumbest thing I could have said. I knew what was going to happen: I was soon going to board a flight to Boston, Massachusetts.

OH THIS STRANGE NUMBER!

Facebook was a popular social networking site among the youth. Interacting online was quickly becoming the most efficient way to get things done – especially from afar. I found a page dedicated to international students, and I posted a question about housing options close to the University. Shortly thereafter, I received a message from a girl named Christine Flake – the first American girl to ever send me a Facebook message. I read her reply expectantly, but found no answers. *"Hi and Congratulations!"* was pretty much all she had to say, which was sweet, and I appreciated the gesture. But I still needed to know where I'd rest my head upon arrival. With a little more research, I found the Graduate Indian Student Association (GISA), and was told that Ron was the Head of GISA. I thought, *Ron! An American leading an Indian community? Interesting.*

The next day, my phone flashed. I picked it up to see who it was, and a strange, seemingly impossible number appeared on the screen. Who could this be?

"Hello?" I asked, tentatively.

"Hi, is this Kartik?"

"Yes." I stood up. It sounded important.

"Hey Kartik, this is Ron." He said, cheerfully. I guess I was silent for a second too long, because he continued: "… from the US. From UMass Boston."

"Oh, hi Ron" My voice trembled. Did *he* have the power to revoke my passage to the US?

"Congratulations, man, on your admission!" Okay. So it's still on. Great.

"Thanks Ron, and thanks for your call!"

"No problem man. So you're looking for housing facilities?"

"Yes. Yeah."

"Okay, so there are several students coming in your batch. What we do here is we try to accommodate newbies in our apartments, initially, while they look for their own place. You're welcome to stay with us for few days."

"Thank you, Sir!" I habitually said *Sir*, instead of just *Ron*.

"What date are you flying out?"

"The 20th of August, Sir"

"Great! Send me your itinerary and I'll come pick you up at the airport." That was very thoughtful. Did they do that for all the new students? I thanked him and then remembered I hadn't been able to find him on Facebook.

"Oh! Are you on Facebook?"

"Of course. Don't know many people who aren't these days!"

"I know, right? It's just…I couldn't find you, so…"

"Ah, yes. My full name is Ronak Shah. That's where you'll find me."

Ohh *Gujju*?! I thought to myself. *He's not American, after all!* "Excellent, I will find you there. Thanks again for the call, man. I look forward to meeting you!"

"Same here…have a safe flight!"

And with that, he was gone. I felt much better knowing I wasn't going to arrive blind. I wondered, though, could a person find an apartment in just a few days? I suddenly had so many questions that I should have asked while I had him on the phone. Oh well, I guess that's what Facebook is for.

9

THE LAST EXPRESSIONS

It was August. I had only three days left in Indore, after which I'd spend ten days in Ratlam, and on the tenth day I'd take a flight from Mumbai to Boston. So much to do before I boarded that plane! Sonia and I went on a little shopping spree to get me ready for this new chapter in my life.

Walking the long stretch of the mall, glaring into shop windows I suddenly wished I'd prowled the Internet to find out what was fashionable over there. "What do people wear in the US, do you think?" Sonia shrugged. "What kind of bags do you think they use? Belts? Wallets?" I looked at Sonia, but she was clearly lost in thought. I wondered whether I should continue my search for a nice shirt, or ask her what she was thinking. I figured she would tell me when she was ready, so I took her hand and pulled her into a store that caught my eye. My budget was limited, and I had to make sure to get the necessities first. I'd read a comment on Facebook that said: "If you're coming to Boston, be sure to get a thick jacket and at least fifteen pairs of underwear."

Do people soil themselves in Boston? I thought. Perhaps it's so cold that your undergarments freeze and you need a back-up pair available at all times. I wasn't a big fan of doing laundry, so I decided to double up and get 30. Just to be safe. One thing was for sure – they'd be cheaper here than in the States, so better to get them now.

The bags started piling up. I bought everything from hair oil to slippers and as I left the mall, I looked like a wholesaler of clothes and household items. I could've opened my own store right then and there.

On my last day in Indore, Sonia and I wanted to spend every moment together, as we didn't know when we would see each other again. We went, of course, to *Shake & Bake* to reminisce, and grabbed our patented corner table.

"You'll probably forget me when you get there," Sonia said. There were three possibilities: this was a moment of insecurity, the beginning of one of our sarcastic banter sessions, or a test. I figured I'd play it safe.

"C'mon Soni, how can you say that?"

"Soon you will find a blond girl who looks at you with fluttering eyes, and you won't be able to resist." Surely this was sarcastic banter. I joined in.

"Well, sure, if she's hot…who can resist a blond batting her lashes?" I let out a little laugh to let her know I was joining her sarcasm.

She pushed her plate towards me, "So you won't miss me?"

"No, because I'll find *you* in all the girls I meet."

"That's not funny."

It *was* test and I failed.

"When will you come back?"

There was a tremble of sadness on her face. Although I had decided to keep my responses casual and non-committal, seeing that made me drop the sarcasm and my tone turned to one more direct and endearing. "Very soon honey. I will try to come back for a visit within a year." I realized that I really didn't know when I'd come back. A trip like that would be expensive. I really would try, though. Sonia averted her eyes from me, and I could tell they were about to well up with tears.

"Hey Soni, what happened," I asked with all the concern I could muster at that moment.

I noticed a lone crystal of a teardrop making its way over the eyelashes and down her cheeks, onto the nape of her neck. She held my hand and with all due emotions she said: "Kartik, it will not be possible for me to live without you. Wherever I go in this city, I will miss you. All these places and moments are tied to you. I can't imagine my life without you. I put my trust in you and I expect that same trust on your side – wherever you live."

Her words shook me. She seemed completely broken. The scene became intense, and made me realize that the step I was taking might not be as easy as I thought.

I held her face with both hands, "Soni, you are my first love. You have become an indispensable part of my life. I will miss you terribly: all the things you've done for me, the love and care you give me every day. Who will be there to see me struggling and offer a shoulder, or gently laugh at me to put things in perspective? Most importantly, who will I share my dessert with now?" That made her smile, and my heart sank at the realization that I wouldn't see that smile every day. It was suddenly hitting me. I'd been so excited for this new adventure; I barely gave myself time to think about the things I would miss.

"I will miss seeing you," I continued, "seeing your smile and making you laugh when you're sad. I know I'm the one leaving, but I'm leaving the most important part of my life behind, and it's equally as painful for me. My success is incomplete without you. Without you it's like a flower with no fragrance, a season without rain, or a heart without feelings. Just two years and we will be together again. I promise."

My words seemed to calm her, like a fast-acting pill that dissolves under your tongue. But the truth remained, and she wouldn't let me forget it, that I wasn't going to be around to hold her in my arms. After that heartfelt discussion, it was time to go to the train station. My sendoff felt incomplete without the presence of two other people, so I made a conference call to Kabeer, and Raghu:

"Bros! I'm at the station…leaving our second home town!"

"Oh man! Great, but sad," Raghu said. I knew he'd be the only one to express true emotion and not cover it up with sarcasm.

"I already miss your dirty, stinky bed sheets." Kabeer joked.

"Haha, and I will miss your mosquito-killing deodorants," I said, with a little more sincerity than I'd planned.

"Okay, thanks man. Well, I guess this goodbye. For now."

"I never thought the day would come when we'd separate," Raghu's voice was full of emotions. Naturally, Kabeer fixed the situation with another joke.

"Just remember one thing," he said. "Keep your room clean, otherwise they will throw you out of the house. I endured your disaster for four years, but those Americans may not be as accommodating."

"Don't worry, I'll just teach them how to keep the place dirty!" they laughed.

"Hey, and if you want me to hack some exams, let me know. I still have contacts in the US. I got your back, bro," Kabeer said.

"Absolutely! How else will I pass my classes?" All jokes aside, I needed to get back to Sonia. I could tell she was getting anxious. "Okay, peeps," I said. "I have to go. My next call will be from an international number!"

"Ok, sexy," Kabeer said. "Take care bro…good luck!"

We all said goodbye, and as I hung up, I felt a real pang of sadness. I was really going to miss my buddies.

Sonia and I had fifteen minutes together. It should have been a beautiful, loving, sweet time, but everything seemed blank. It felt like we were both in a choke-hold with nothing left to say. She wept as the train whistled. I held her in my arms, tight.

"Please come back soon. I love you." Her last words were muted, as she buried her head in the crook of my shoulder.

"I love you too. I promise, I will come back very soon… Do one thing for me?"

We loosened our grip on each other just enough so she could look at me. With our arms still around each other, I simply said, "Stay happy; stay blessed." And with that, I kissed her one last time and got on the train.

A TOUGH MOMENT

Those ten days at home before my departure to the US were the richest days of my life. Apparently, there is quite a high importance placed on a person when they are about to leave for a relatively undetermined period of time. Everyone wanted a piece of me during those ten days. Those otherwise ambiguous to my presence turned particularly helpful.

Even my dad was more courteous and tolerant of my activities than ever before. Normally, even if I'd been in the middle of a television show, he would change the channel to the news or a mythological program. But during those ten days, he actually asked, "Kartik, do you want the remote control?" *Are you ok, Dad?* I thought. I wished he had offered me that several years ago. He wasted countless hours of my time watching all his boring channels. But he was making up for it now. The most astonishing change was that he sat up with us until the wee hours of the night, never demanding that we go to bed, and never asking us to get up early each morning. Miraculous.

Aditi helped with the last-minute shopping and packing. Another miracle. We fought less in those ten days than ever before, but of course we still had our moments. My mom, on the other hand, was extra anxious. She was counting the days and nights, and they seemed to be going too fast for her to keep us. She, of course, had the menu planned for the full ten days, including breakfast, lunch and dinner. She made herself busy in the kitchen, doing nothing but preparing food, as if I might starve to death in the US.

Family friends and relatives came from far and wide to see me before I left, and some of them even invited me to dinner. It was fun to have everyone pamper me. I felt that, perhaps, I should have made it a point to travel abroad regularly - one sure does get the royal treatment when they're going away for a while.

The day finally arrived. My train to Mumbai was in the evening; my luggage was packed to the gills. I was taking everything I could think of. I didn't want to be caught without the necessities and be forced to spend US dollars on something I could've gotten cheaper at home.

My close relatives, including my maternal grandma — the person who loved me the most — visited us on that final day. We all sat in the dining room, my dad on the center couch which was his patented place. The scene was pretty sentimental. My dad took the opportunity to lecture me, addressing some basic warnings and precautions in his usual tone, and telling me in detail all the things to watch out for, as if he'd been there before. Of course, he hadn't.

"Kartik *beta*, you are going to a new country. We don't know anyone there. If anything goes wrong, we might not be able to solve it from here. You must take care of yourself. You are going there to study. Therefore, just study and study. Never deviate from your goals." I already knew most of the things he was going to say, but I allowed him this last hurrah. This was how he showed his love. "Never do anything that may bring shame to you, or to our family. Don't get into criminal activities. Live in a good circle, with good people."

"Yes dad," I said. There wasn't much more to say to that.

"Never drink or smoke. Don't be influenced by the modernity of Western culture."

"Yes dad," I said again. He didn't need to know that some eastern cultures I'd come across included loads of drinking and smoking. Not something that was limited to the Western world.

"More importantly," he continued, "try to avoid girls. Things are quite open there. Be careful."

Now you are kidding, Dad! I thought to myself. I looked at Aditi, she was smiling at our father's ridiculous rant. I gave her a look and her smile grew bigger.

"Take care of your expenses. Don't spend too much on partying and going out. The bank has approved our loan and the more you spend, the more we have to repay."

Okay Dad, I got it. I thought. But he wasn't done.

"And here's the most important thing: never eat non-vegetarian food. Red meat is quite prevalent over there, I've heard. Be careful and remain strict in your vegetarian food habits."

"Yes dad, I will." I waited for him to continue. There had to be another 'most important thing' in there, but he seemed finished, so I took a deep breath.

It was soon time to leave. The car was loaded and I was heading back inside for our final goodbyes when I heard a loud cry from inside. I was sure it was my mom, though it sounded a bit like the cry of a wounded animal. I went back inside and hugged her. "Mom, please stop crying. Don't worry. I will be back soon."

Upon seeing my mother's tears, Aditi also started crying. I, too, got emotional, though I was enjoying the attention. I had never felt this loved in my entire life.

"Take care of yourself," my mom chortled through her tears.

"You too, mom." I said, getting a little choked up myself. "I love you *Maa*," was all I could say.

Finally, I touched everyone's feet and went outside, where Mr. Gupta and neighboring families were waiting to send me off. Mr. Gupta, as per usual, invited me in. I respectfully declined, bidding goodbye.

We drove away as everyone on the street waved goodbye. My family accompanied me to the station, where the train was to come in fifteen minutes. While waiting for the train, I observed my dad. He seemed to have mixed feelings: proud that his son was going to the USA for higher education, yet saddened that he'd be helpless when it came to my needs. I could see that was going to be hard for him.

Finally, the train arrived. I hugged my mom, who was still crying, and said, "Mom, I will come back soon. You take care of your health." I hugged my dad, which I rarely did, and said nothing. I hugged my little love, Aditi, "Take care; I will get you stuff from the US. I never got you anything from Indore, but this is different."

Aditi, with gloomy eyes, said sweetly, "I don't need anything *bhai*, you just take care of yourself."

I got onto the train.

I reached Mumbai the next day and headed straight for the airport. This was going to be my first time on an airplane. Perhaps I should have practiced! A long international flight as my first flight ever might not have been the best idea. But… too late. I was about to board the plane and there was no turning back.

I boarded the flight and was glad to have a window seat. It was sort of my way of getting closure – saying goodbye to an era. As the plane took off, things started getting smaller from the window, and after a few minutes, everything went white as we ascended into the clouds. Kind of a metaphor for life, I mused, as I stared at the blank canvas before me.

We landed in London for a short layover. I stayed on the plane, as it was a short turn-around, and I feared I would miss the flight if I wandered through the airport. I was easily distracted in such places. As people started boarding for this second leg of the journey, I could clearly differentiate the between the crowd that boarded from Mumbai to London, and that which boarded from London to Boston.

PART II

USA AND ITS CHARM

10

THE GRASS ON THE OTHER SIDE

The big day had arrived. I landed, for the first time, on international soil. I was in the USA! – The dream destination for millions like me. I was instructed to stand at a particular booth so that Ron could find me, and I stood there like a little kid who cowers quietly among strangers. After quite a long time, I realized that someone was supposed to pick me up. I thought about calling Ron from a phone booth, but quickly realized I had only Indian coins with me. I pulled my cell phone out of my pocket, wondering if I could make a call before switching over to an American number, when I heard a voice pierce through the air.

"Hey…is that Kartik? UMass?"

I turned to locate the source of this voice and saw someone approach me.

"Yes!" I said, and waved back at him, perhaps a little too eagerly.

"Hey, I am Sid, Ron's batchmate. Welcome!"

"Oh, thanks!" I was being as soft-spoken and well-mannered as I could be.

"Can I help you with your bags?"

"No, I've got it. Thank you, though!"

He led me outside, where he said his car was waiting. There was so much information to process and so much to take in. We stepped out of the airport and my goose bumps turned bone chilling. Boston was COLD! We reached the car, and I was astonished to see a shiny black Toyota Camry. My dream car!

Waiting in the car was the great Ron. I got in the car, and felt immediately out of sorts. The steering was on the left-hand side. I had heard of such differences, but it was quite disconcerting to see it in person. I didn't know if I'd ever get used to that. Ron welcomed me and waited until everything was loaded into the trunk. Then he took off at top speed.

During our car ride, and the conversations that carried on while driving, I could not tear my eyes away from the windows. I wanted to see what my new world looked like but it was dark, so I couldn't see much. Still, I found comfort in the foreign darkness. Just then, a grand Limousine passed right by us. *Wow! That's America.*

"How was the journey?" asked Ron.

"Long!" I said. "And tiring!"

"I know. Damn jet-lag."

"So you are from Indore?" Sid asked.

"Yeah. Actually, I did my engineering there. I am originally from Ratlam."

"Ohh *Ratlami Sev* and *Namkeen?*"

"Haha. Yes, exactly."

"Did you bring any" he enquired, his voice laden with hope that I actually might have.

"If you open my bags, you'd find more snacks than clothes!"

They laughed. I guess my sense of humor did translate into English.

"Sid sir and Ron sir, where are you fr–"

"Oh please, don't call us sir. No one says that here!" Ron interrupted.

My stomach tightened for a second. I was already doing things wrong. These new customs were going to take a little getting used to, and I just had to learn as I went.

"Okay," I said. "Good to know. Sorry."

"Great. I have a lot of questions for you!"

"Newbies always do," Sid said. "Don't worry, you have come to the right place – you'll be staying at 'The President's' apartment." Sid patted Ron.

"Wow…!" I couldn't help but voice my astonishment. No one seemed to notice.

"Do you know a guy named Jatin Desai, from Ahmedabad?" asked Sid.

"The guy who was trying to bargain the room rent?" I asked, with an edge of biting sarcasm in my voice.

"Ha ha, yeah," Sid had also noticed his nickel-and-diming nature. "He is also landing tonight. He will stay at our place for a few days."

The conversation continued, and finally we arrived at our destination. The place looked beautiful and clean from the outside. The entry way was adorned with a fancy, intricate carpet, and I thought for a moment that they were putting me up in some luxury hotel. When we entered the apartment, they lit a cigarette at the window. I had seen Ron's photo on Facebook, but I couldn't honestly recognize him in person.

For some reason, I felt a little intimidated by him. Maybe because they called him 'The President,' or perhaps, because he was the only one who had any real expectations of me.

"I'm grateful to have found out about GISA …and its great president, of course."

"Great? I don't know why people chose me…" Ron tried to downplay his position.

Sid looked at me and with a completely serious look on his face said: "Yeah, even I don't know how that happened."

They gave each other a high five and started laughing. They seemed to be very close friends.

"You deserve it," I said. "You helped me without even knowing me."

"That's just how it works around here. Someone helped me, I helped you, and you will help someone tomorrow. It's a cycle." He shrugged as he spoke, again downplaying his role, and moved the conversation into the living room. He and Sid sat on the couch, and I sat in the comfy leather chair across from them.

"Where are you from?" I asked Ron, not remembering if we'd discussed that in one of our phone conversations.

"I am basically a *Gujju* but born and brought up in Pune."

"Oh, I love Pune! It's full of youth, fashion and energy."

"Agreed!" Ron said with a proud smile.

Ron embodied the quintessential Pune-born kid. He looked like a model and he carried himself with admirable confidence. You couldn't help but like the guy.

"And you studied Engineering, right?" I asked, searching for commonalities to help us connect.

"No bro. I got my Bachelors in Finance from London."

"Oh, London? Wow!" No wonder I detected a British accent! "I have it in my head that the only people who apply to schools in the US are engineers, so I just thought…"

"I know, it's such a cliché. Those who don't know what to do with their life are happened to be them."

"Haha. You're so right." And then I turned to Sid. "And you're from?" I asked.

"Bangalore!" he replied, seemingly displeased with this fact.

"The Silicon Valley of India. It's a fascinating city with so much opportunity, right?!" I said.

"Indeed. But I should have come here sooner."

"The US has even better opportunities for the IT world." I thought it to be a known fact.

"No man, it's the land of opportunity for beer lovers," he said, laughing at his own joke.

We all laughed, and then there was a lull in the conversation. I didn't know what to say next. "Bro, you had a long journey. If you want to freshen up, the bathroom is down the hall to the right," Ron offered.

"Thanks!" I said, taking my cue and exiting with my toiletry bag.

As I opened the bathroom door, I was shocked by the clean, shiny interior. No more wet, grimy tiles but fluffy bathroom rugs; no buckets but a nice cozy bathtub; no more mugs in the toilet but toilet paper and no more insects like cockroaches and lizards. The cleanliness scared me a little.

As it was almost a twenty-four hour journey, I thought taking a shower would be a bright idea. Since everything around me was too sophisticated or looked complicated, I happily took out my favorite bar of Lux soap and turned on the shower. The adjustable water temperature and the endless flow of water were soothing. After the fresh shower, I began to unpack a little and arrange my stuff, which caused an image of my dad's face to pop into my head. "Keep things in their own places," he'd always say. I suddenly remembered I needed to call them, to let them know I'd arrived safely, so I asked Sid if I could use the phone.

"Sure, but don't tell them how we are!" he joked. "No need to worry them."

"Haha. That's for sure," I grinned knowingly as I replied, and he showed me how to make calls to India.

My dad picked up with a booming, anxious voice.

"Kartik *bete*, it is good to hear from you. Did you reach safe? Did they come to pick you up?"

"Yes dad, they did. I arrived safe and sound."

"What's your plan now? Will you see the university today?"

As my life had changed, so had the clock. I explained to my dad it was 11:00 PM.

"Oh, is it? It is 8:00 in the morning here!"

Always sensitive to the cost of things, he quickly handed the phone to my mom. I'm sure you can guess what her burning questions were: Food and safety. My mom never seemed to think beyond this. This was her world.

After hanging up with my parents, I was walking out of the room when the image of Sonia, saying *"Bhool gaye na mujhe?"* popped into my head. Oh no, we can't have that. I quickly dialed her number. She bombarded me with questions but didn't give me time to answer them. She was worried. Not sure why, clearly I was alive and well and able to dial a phone. I calmed her down as I described my journey in a nutshell, and told her I'd call her back as soon as I get my own phone line.

"How long will *that* be?" I could hear the tears building up in her throat.

"I don't know, Soni…a few days, maybe." And with that, we got off the phone. I felt bad for her. My life was changing exponentially while the only thing she had to hang on to was her old routine. When I came out of the room, there were three unfamiliar pieces of luggage. I looked up to discover we'd had a new arrival.

A boy with semi-fair skin and short dark hair extended his hand. "I am Jatin Desai," he said. Oh! This was the famous Facebook guy who tried to negotiate the rent. Can't blame him for trying, I guess. "I am from Gujarat," he said, putting a not-so-subtle emphasis on Gujarat… and why not? All *Gujjus* think of Gujarat as the branded state. He wore a thick gold chain around his neck, an oversized gold watch on his wrist, and a number of gold rings on his fingers. So much gold!

"*Kemchho?*" Ron asked. No conversation with a *Gujju* could start without saying *Kemchho*.

"*Majama!*" He replied.

Jatin was born into a *Gujju* family, and brought up in Ahmedabad. His dad was a *Gujarati* and mom was a *Sindhi*. It's a bit of a frightening combination: *Gujju*, who can never spend a penny and *Sindhi*, who never miss an opportunity to earn a penny.

The apartment was a mess filled with people and luggage, and then Sid returned to add to the clutter.

"How many students have come in, in your batch?" Sid asked Jatin.

"Around twenty, I guess. Most of them have already arranged permanent housing."

"As far as I know, four of the girls booked a two-bedroom apartment.

At the mention, I felt a little pang in my stomach. *When can we meet them?*

"There is one guy, Satya, who booked a two-bedroom apartment." Sid said, consulting the Facebook page.

"Hey, you might want to check with him. If he hasn't already found roommates, you could maybe live there," Ron said, trying to be helpful, and at the same time letting it be known that we would not be welcomed there for *too* long. I understood the house was full.

"We can talk about this later. You guys must be hungry! Come into the kitchen and have some food," Sid invited us to eat.

I was curious to know how people in the US ate. I was always taught that burgers and pizza were the staple food. Burgers were, of course, out of the question. "Die, but never touch non-vegetarian food there!" my dad had warned me. I wondered what they would offer me.

Sid clapped and then hooted out to us "Guys c'mon we have cooked special *chicken biryani* and *egg bhurji.*"

My nerves leaped into my throat. I was completely choked.

I swallowed hard to clear the nerves and smiled. "Actually," I said as sweetly as possible. "I don't eat non-veg."

"What?" Sid's wide eyes landed on me. "How are you still alive?"

"I…don't know. I've just never eaten meat. I've been a vegetarian all my life."

"Oh, really? Trust me. If you haven't had chicken, you haven't lived."

Ron, who was also (fortunately) a vegetarian, came to my rescue. "C'mon guys, don't start shoving your crappy philosophy down his throat. Kartik, of course we have vegetarian options. What will you have?" I was relieved to find Ron vegetarian.

"Anything would be fine." I shrugged. *As long as it's not meat*, I thought.

He got some frozen *chapatis, stuffed parathas*, and vegetable curries out of the freezer. I watched as he put the *chapatis and parathas* in a heated pan. He then put the curries in a bowl and put them in the microwave. Five minutes later we were sitting down to eat.

"Oh wow! That was fast!" They could see I was shocked.

"Yeah, food in the US is fast and frozen. Especially for students!"

Who knew we could prepare a meal from freezer to fork in the blink of an eye?

Jatin filled his plate with biryani and bhurji and started stuffing his face as if he hadn't been given food for weeks. I found my ready-to-eat food to be pretty good. After finishing, Sid asked us to rinse the plates and put them in the dishwasher. I had seen dishwashers before, in India, but never saw them working quite the way they should. By now it was quite late. With full bellies, we were ready to call it a night. Ron gave us blankets and comforters, and we set up our sleeping quarters in the living room for the night. We tried to sleep, but suddenly we weren't all that sleepy all of a sudden. Damn jet-lag!

"You awake too?" I whispered.

"Wide awake." Jatin complained.

"So…What's your major?" I asked.

"Finance. Yours?"

"Anything but IT. I will decide later."

We both sat up and decided that trying to sleep was futile.

"Question for you: have you looked for a part-time job?" he asked, suddenly changing the topic. Where there is a *Sindhi*, there is a desire to earn.

"No. I don't really know much about how and where I can search for jobs."

"We're in the same boat, then. You know, if we get a job, we can cover monthly expenses and be able to put some savings aside as well."

Savings? I thought. *I've never had a savings account in my life!* Where there is a *Gujju*, there is a savings-and-investment plan. I suddenly understood why he had opted for a major in Finance. "Let's see tomorrow in the GISA meeting. Ron might give some insights about how to find a job, etc.," I said.

"Good idea. By the way, how much are you looking to pay for rent?" His tone sounded more humming and mysterious in the late-night silence, as if he was planning to rob a bank.

"I'm not sure. I don't even know how much things are going for around here. I want to try and pay as little as possible for a decent apartment. Those are my only parameters," I answered, matching his bank-robbing tone.

"I was thinking the same thing," he said. "We could try to find a place together. Maybe we could get a good deal."

"Sounds good to me!" I said. One of the best attributes of Jatin was his power to negotiate. The discussion continued for some time, but basically stayed focused on one theme: MONEY!

Around 5 AM, I finally drifted to sleep. I wanted to be well-rested for the GISA meet-up in the morning, where all the new students and second-years are introduced to each other... but it was too late for well-rested. I had to settle for a few short hours of shut-eye.

11

WAIT! IS THAT *OUR* CAMPUS?

The next morning (and officially a week before the start of the semester) I opened the GISA page on Facebook to remind and re-familiarize myself with some of the people I'd be meeting. I had been keeping an eye on two of the people in particular: Natasha Malhotra and Shalini Rangnathan. They seemed the most attractive amongst the new students, and it seemed I wasn't the only one who thought so. They had a whole lot of replies on each of their posts – more so than many of the others, ha…ha. We made our way to the meet-up, and walked along Harbor Point Bayside on our way to University Bayside. Harbor Point Residential Community was a five-minute walk from the university, and Bayside was a paved path connecting and encircling the two. Wherever you went, you got the breathtaking view of the Atlantic Ocean. No wonder UMass, Boston was considered one of the most beautiful campuses in the U.S. It was awe-inspiring. The panoramic greenery included sweet-gum trees and beautifully cut grass. The grass *is* greener on the other side! The Boston skyline was clearly visible, and looked as if shining pearls had been scattered over the water. If you walked alone on this path, you'd get lost in the silence of your thoughts. If you walked with someone, conversations would be a little deeper and emotions a little more raw. It made you see things you might not otherwise see.

An acquaintance of mine wrote a little poem about that path, and I couldn't agree more:

> *The Journey is incomplete without a walk here;*
>
> *Conversations are empty without sharing here;*
>
> *No cologne is more refreshing than the air here.*

Our new batch gathered for a casual meet at the Bayside walk in front of the University. Many of us had been introduced on Facebook and were now meeting for the first time. It felt odd to recognize complete strangers. The most common question was, "Where are you from?" Nine times out of ten they were from one of three places: Gujarat, Andhra Pradesh or Chennai. I was in the lonely ten percent NOT from any of those places.

"What's your major?" was the second-most frequently asked question. You could easily discern the MBA students from the MS students. MBA hopefuls were ostentatiously talkative, while MS first-years tended to be more reserved, and intellectual introverts.

Ron was a great orator. He shared information about the best courses, the best supermarkets, the best bars, and other important college town information. The entire crowd perked up even further as he said, "And now I want to tell a little bit about part-time jobs and assistantships." Everyone seemed to have a "fuck, yeah" attitude about that one…anything to keep them from having to ask their relatives for money.

Ron's spiel ended and we mingled a bit more. The circle of people I had met was very different from my Indore clan; a more diverse group, from one coast to another and more notably, we were speaking nothing but English. For me, it was a little overwhelming to carry on a conversation in English alone, so I chose to listen more than to speak. At one point, Jatin and I were standing next to each other, taking a bit of a break from the mayhem, when we saw a guy saunter up and stand next to us. He was quite fashionable, wearing a backward cap, gold bracelet, and big round watch. I couldn't help but notice the giant tattoo on his arm.

"Hey," he said, as he stretched out his hand. "I am Mohit Khanna."

"I am Kartik. Nice to meet you."

"I am JD, Jatin Desai."

I shot Jatin a look. He looked into my eyes, winked, and said, "Yes, JD"

He loved to be called so. Since then he was JD for us.

"Where are you from?" I asked Mohit.

"I am from Delhi. We have a family business, on a large scale for many decades, so we have been there for many generations."

JD and I shot a knowing look at each other as if to say, "Typical *Delhite*, offering up information that would boost his status and ego." Another guy joined us. He looked very simple and decent in a stitched shirt and pants. "Hi," he said as he approached. "I am Ramprasad Venkatesh Balsubramanyam."

I'm sorry, what?

"You can just call me Ram," he said, smiling knowingly.

Oh, thank God! I thought.

"I am from Chennai," he said in a very thick accent, over-articulating every syllable. "Did you enroll for the courses?" He asked, his accent still thick. "No man...why the rush?" Mohit answered, in between chomps as he masticated a piece of chewing gum.

Ram looked scared. "Only two days left."

"Have you enrolled, then?" I asked.

"Oh yes," he beamed, "a month ago."

Just then, another guy wearing a shiny long-sleeved yellow shirt joined the conversation. We were becoming quite the popular group, it would seem.

"I am Satya Gullapalli from Jangaon near Hyderabad," he introduced himself.

"Oh nice," Mohit said, lighting up for the first time. "Do you know a place called *Kukanaka* nearby?"

"Oh. Well, no."

"Even I don't...haha!" Mohit laughed alone.

While we were chatting, I saw JD looking around and I spotted a group of girls behind us at his sight. He winked at me.

Running short of time, Ron's voice came splicing through the air.

"We will now be moving on to the University. Tour time!"As we approached the first leg of our tour, we saw a huge eleven-story building in front of us. My eyes grew wide…this was way bigger than our building at the engineering college!"

"Friends this is our library," Sid announced.

My jaw dropped. The library? If this was the library, how big was the entire university? He continued: "The campus has a separate building for each subject: sciences, commerce, arts, management, administration and more" I started walking faster, overcome with excitement. Some of the others seemed to share my astonishment, while others were un-phased. We reached the food court. It was almost the size of a cricket field in my college.

"This is one of six cafes on campus," Ron beamed. "This one is my personal favorite."

"Six?" I blurted out as my eyes became even wider. This one café was like seventeen *Shake & Bake*, and this was only one of SIX! We finally reached the building that lured us to the United States in the first place: The College of Management. For me, **it was a dream come true.** All the classrooms were tech savvy with projectors and wall-mounted monitors, and there were lockers in the corridors – the kind I used to see in Hollywood movies.

During the tour, the second-years spoke more about the essentials, spouting facts about education in the US, dispelling myths, and assuaging fears. The vibe of this group, this university, this level of education, felt very different to me. It was no longer a race against each other, but a game of challenging yourself and exceeding your own expectations. No mom or dad would come and push you. You can cheat, but you'd only be cheating yourself.

All in all, it took us five hours to cover the entire campus. After the tour, we were ready for a nap. People slowly started to disperse, but Mohit, Jatin and I were still standing together.

"Have you guys looked for an apartment yet? I am currently staying at a very expensive hotel," Mohit bragged.

Oh c'mon, *Delhite*, nobody asked you.

"No, actually," JD answered. "Hey, Kartik, you remember Ron told us that Satya has leased an apartment? We should talk to him."

Speak of the devil, just then Satya walked up. "Hey Kartik, I came to know you and Jatin are looking for an apartment," he said as he approached.

"True," I said, hoping he'd make the offer.

"I leased a two-bedroom apartment and I am looking for the roommates. Why don't you have a look?"

"That would be great," I said, pleased that I didn't have to ask. "Hey, Khanna, you should join us." We already started calling by his surname.

The four of us went to see the apartment. He showed us around as if he were a tour guide. He wore a small *tilak* on the forehead, and a bead in a thread chain around his neck, which appeared to have some sort of religious significance. "I try to keep the apartment clean," he said. My hiccups started.

After a while, JD managed to ask the question: "Just out of curiosity, how much is the rent?" "Only $1600 a month! It's a good apartment. The three of you could move in," said Satya.

"We'll think about it and let you know," JD said. We left the apartment and headed back towards Ron's place. "What do you think guys?" JD asked, barely out of the earshot of Satya's apartment.

"Not a bad deal," I said, "but I foresee a huge problem."

"What?" He stopped in his tracks and looked at me "The apartment was insanely clean"

JD laughed. "Don't worry, we will bring it down to your level."

"Deal!" I responded, grinning.

"What about you, Khanna?"

"Yeah, it's only $1600 dude. Even if it had been $2000, it would have been worth it," he said, chewing his gum.

Fucking grandiloquent.

Two days later we moved in to the new apartment.

"Keep coming for Chicken Biryani, dude," Sid said as we were heading out the door. He shot JD a quick wink.

"Absolutely," JD said, glad to accept the offer. "Best biryani in town!"

Ron looked at me and said, "Don't worry bro, you can keep coming for *Paneer Tikka.*"

"Will do!" I said. "Thanks for all of your help. Truly." And with that, the three of us moved in with Satya for a new beginning.

12

NEW ACCENTS, NEW FACES – THE ORIENTATION DAY

Getting an education abroad is not just about being in a foreign country, but actually, interacting with the people there as well. The day after we moved, we had to attend orientation – all newly admitted international students were required to appear. Beforehand, I went back to Facebook and found a different page dedicated to all the new students at the university. The group was not restricted to Indians, but included students from all over the globe. Exciting!

My housemates and I reached the Ball Room, the venue where the event was being held, and I instantly felt the fresh energy and excitement in the room. The diversity in the room was a beautiful thing. Hundreds of students in a variety of shades; it was a multicultural Mecca. The chancellor, deans from every department, and the management staff and professors were all present.

Someone walked onto the stage and the room went from bustling hubbub to nearly silent in the matter of seconds. "Hello to all the bright new students and future graduates," Chancellor William Story began. "We welcome you to the International Society of Global Education!" I felt honored to be among them, a rare moment indeed. Other staff members got up, and offered general information about the academics and facilities provided by the university. When the boring lecture was over, we were able to mingle and interact. I introduced myself to the two pretty girls sitting next to me. They had the loveliest skin – smooth like butter. I mustered the old charm, bravery, and communication skills and went for it.

"Hi, I am Kartik Jain."

It looked as though they didn't understand, so I repeated myself, but simplified it to just my first name.

"Ohh, Khat –tik. Hello, I am Fu."

I waited for her to go on, but it turns out that was her entire first name.

"Fu Li," she continued in the silence. "Nice to meet you."

Fu Li. Short and sweet. "Nice to meet you, too, Fu." I giggled inwardly at the rhyme I'd just made, but she remained oblivious to my little joke. "I am Jing Zhang," the second girl bowed her head a little as she said her name.

"Where are you from?" I asked.

"Beijing, China," Fu answered, as she pointed to herself.

"And me Shenzhen, China," Jing answered with that same subtle bowing of the head. It was less of a bow and more of a half-nod I guess. "You are from India?" she guessed.

"You know your neighbors very well!" I replied, and they laughed. Good start.

We talked a bit, and as it turned out, they were both there for an MBA in Finance. When it came out that I was in IT, Fu said, "If you don't mind me asking, why all Indians in IT?"

"For the same reason all products are *Made in China.*"

"Haha… smart," Fu laughed.

We had a good conversation, but agreed that we needed to socialize and meet more people. We said our goodbyes and hope-to-see-you-laters and were on our way.

I met a few more students with strange names from a variety of countries before I joined JD, who was eyeing the food table. I scanned the unknown delicacies, expecting to find some delicious vegetarian options. I found nothing but salad. I got jealous looking at JD's plate, as he piled it with chicken sandwiches. Instantly my Dad's face flashed before my eyes. I served myself some salad. We started walking away from the food, towards the tables that were set up for us to eat and interact.

The next thing I knew we were face-to-face with two beautiful girls, bumping them lightly. I felt like I was in high school again. I could even feel myself blush.

"Oh, sorry!" they both said, smiling. As if they'd rehearsed it or something.

"No problem at all," JD said, and then suavely transitioned into an introduction. "Hi. I'm Jatin. How are you?"

"I'm good," said the girl who had bumped arms with JD. "I am Natasha."

"And I am Shalini," the other one piped in. "Good to meet you."

As luck would have it, they happened to be the two gorgeous girls I had noticed on the bay side during the GISA meet-up. Hello again, ladies.

"I am Kartik. Nice to meet to you!" I said, as I nervously shook hands with both of them.

"Where are you from?" asked JD.

"I am from Chandigarh," said Natasha. She carried herself with a type of confidence I hadn't seen in many girls of her age. My stomach started fluttering. "I am from Hyderabad," said Shalini, interrupting my fantasy. As my focus changed to Shalini, I saw that she was even more beautiful than her Facebook profile picture appeared. I was about to say something to that effect when JD jumped in.

"I am from Ahmedabad," he said. "And KJ…I mean Kartik here, is from Indore. But originally from Ratlam, isn't that right, KJ?"

Oh *KJ*, so now he's speaking on my behalf. Who am I, Helen Keller? I can speak for myself, thank you very much. "Chandigarh is the most beautiful and well-designed city," JD said. Not wanting to leave Shalini out, he added, "And Hyderabad is also glamorous!" He flirted silently for a moment, and then came up with his pick-up line. "You are both perfect representations of your respective cities."

Good God! Would someone please shut this guy up?!

"I have been to Ahmedabad once," Natasha said. "Every other shop sold regional snacks - *Dhokla* and *Fafda, right?*"

JD's smile was so wide I could see teeth that weren't even there. "Just like every other girl in Chandigarh is beautiful, right?"

Oh God! I couldn't stand to hear another blatant pick-up line. "So…" I said, trying to change the subject. "Are you all set with housing?"

Shalini became impatient. "Yeah, we're all set with housing," she said, "but I need a cell phone badly. It feels like I'm totally disconnected from the world."

"We're going Downtown tomorrow to get cell phones," JD blurted out, without hesitation. "Why don't you both join us?"

I hate to admit it, but that was a smart, impromptu idea. This guy might be smoother than I'd like to give him credit for.

The two girls looked at each other and seemed to make a silent decision. "Yeah sure, we'll go," Shalini said, and with that, we bid them goodbye and continued to mingle.

We met a few more students, but no one quite as noteworthy as our future cellphone-buying companions. On the way home after orientation Satya threw a wrench in our plans.

"I really need a cell phone. It feels like I'm disconnected from the world!" Satya whined.

I turned, wanting to say, *Hey, that's exactly what Shalini said!* But JD beat me to the punch. "So what?" he said. "Life is better when you can unplug."

I was completely taken aback by that statement. He was like a social chameleon.

"I already have got two iPhones from India with international sim cards," Khanna flaunted.

"Oh wow! So you need not struggle to go and buy. You lucky man!" JD smoothly boycotted him.

"But I feel like I need to get one soon or I'm gonna go crazy. Let's go tomorrow!" Satya wasn't leaving the trunk.

JD and I, in disappointed stereo said, "Tomorrow?"

"Why? What happened?"

"Nothing. Sure, yeah, we can go tomorrow," I said. *"Never mind that you'll ruin our boy:girl ratio!"* JD said with a glance, but kept his mouth shut. If we were going to be successful roommates, we couldn't start by shutting them out of our plans, even if that meant thwarting our mojo.

13

GADGETS & AMERICA

It seems that every city in the US has a heart called downtown, and Boston was no different. We have such places in our cities as well, those roads where one side of which is lined with retail shops, restaurants, and sometimes theatres too. The five of us walked to the closest metro station, known in Boston as 'The T,' which was a mile from Harbor Point.

The entire ticketing process was quite fancy unlike the one's I was used to in India. Instead of ticket windows there were automatic ticketing machines - something like an ATM, except you put money in rather than take it out. *Guess I'll never have the chance to travel without a ticket,* I thought to myself. *That's disappointing.* I paid for a two-way ticket and got through the doors into the station. Shortly thereafter, the train pulled up and as the doors opened, I found myself in awe once again. The train was speckled with just a few people, and there were more seats than people. Most of the passengers were engrossed in their own thing: reading a book or accessing their mobiles unlike on the train from Ratlam to Indore where passengers would constantly stare at you during the entire journey, as if they had smoked an entire bag of weed before boarding the train. Natasha sat next to me making the journey more exciting, and I had something – someone – to focus on. As I looked, taking my eyes off my shoes, about to engage Natasha in conversation, I caught a glimpse of a sexy blonde girl reading a book across the train. JD must have seen her, too, because I watched as he wriggled his way into the seat right next to her. No accident there.

We arrived at our Downtown stop and emerged from The T. Downtown Boston and it was stunning! We began walking, not really knowing where we were going, but trusting that we'd run into the AT&T store in no time.

"I don't know what phone to get!" Shalini exclaimed as we walked down the street, window-shopping and observing passers-by.

"I'm gonna get the iPhone 4," Natasha said, "I hear it's pretty cheap in the US."

Satya and I looked at each other. *Cheap?* Either they didn't know the price of an iPhone 4, or they were too rich to care.

"What you will get KJ?" JD asked.

My sturdy Nokia 1100 flashed my mind. It's the only phone I'd ever had, and it did the job well. "I'm not really picky," I answered, trying to act casual about the whole thing. I'd most likely get the cheapest one possible.

We reached the AT&T store and were immediately approached by an eager store clerk who, despite his towering stature, had a baby-face that made him look like he was twelve. He explained the two-year contract, and let us in on the fact that with the contract, one could get a phone for less than one-third the retail price. For example, a smartphone worth $600 would cost you just $200. And of course that meant, to me, that a cheaper phone with a two-year contract would cost zero. Now that was an amount I could get on board with. I started looking for phones with a $0 tag, but the iPhone beckoned me. Ah! Why were Apple's products so alluring?

Natasha without question bought her iPhone. JD got one too. *I couldn't believe that this cheapo who was willing to live in a trash can, if it meant paying less rent, actually splurged on an iPhone!* Natasha and JD raised a toast with their iPhones and he smiled. *Mission accomplished.*

Shalini got the Samsung Galaxy S3. A nice phone, for sure, but it was no iPhone. She seemed to be happy with it, though. I had to make a decision, and I was lost in thought when Satya came over and asked if I'd decided.

"I'm so confused," I said.

"Hey, the iPhone is the iPhone man, there's no comparison." "Oh, I know. Is it on you?" I joked.

"Yeah, it's expensive. I get it. Hey, what if we don't eat out for few days?"

I pondered this statement for all of a millisecond before blurting out, "Yeah that sounds like a good plan."

So there it was – our crazy stupid justification to join the masses and get an iPhone for $200. I may never eat out again.

With phones in hand, our next task was to buy laptops. You can't be a student and not own a laptop. "Shall we move on to the Apple store?" JD asked. Actually, it was more of a statement, rather than a question.

"Yeah let's start," said the others. Satya and I exchanged frightened looks. They *were buying electronic gadgets as if they were produced from a grocery store!*

We reached the Apple store, a sprawling three-story building made entirely of glass, which seemed to take up an entire city block. I felt like I'd arrived at Electronic Disneyland. We were immediately approached by an Apple store genius who was ready, willing and able to help us with all our needs.

"Hi, I am Angelina," she said with a cute smile and a quick, subtle wink. She made me melt but the prices made me sure I could not give her my credit card. "I'm just gonna look around," I said to her with as much confidence I could muster.

Satya found me in the kid's corner, sitting on a beanbag with my eyes closed. I was gonna figure this out if it was the last thing I did. You can't be a student without a laptop. And it's not a laptop if it's not a MacBook.

"What do you think?" he asked, knowing how difficult this was. We were in the same boat, he and I. "We're already gonna be living on Cup-O-Noodles and Frozen *parathas* for the next month or so."

"Yeah. How about if we don't get furniture for a few months? This beanbag is actually pretty comfy and I'm sure it's not that expensive. It could be our couch-bed-chair for the whole semester."

"Sounds like a plan!" he laughed, knowing that it was just another crazy justification that we may well regret sooner rather than later. He held out his hand to help me out of the beanbag.

We went straight up to Angelina and said, "We will take two MacBooks, please." And her gorgeous smile was worth every penny.

The five of us, excitedly embracing our new laptops, left the place with a spring in our step as we moved on to the next errand: opening bank accounts at the Bank of America. It couldn't get more American than Apple and BoA.

By the time we got back to Harbor Point, it was evening. We said goodbye to Natasha and Shalini (but not before exchanging our new phone numbers!) and headed back to our temporary residence when I experienced a moment of major culture shock.

It was dark when we reached our block. My two roomies had already crossed the road, but I was still on the other side. While crossing, I saw a car coming from a distance so of course I stopped in my tracks. Since childhood I had been taught that the bigger (and faster) the vehicle, the more right of way it had. The car in question stopped abruptly about ten feet away from me. I wasn't sure why, or what I should do, so I just stood there. Was he looking for something? Did he want to rob me? The vehicle did not move. I squinted and tried to look beyond the headlights. Finally, as my eyes adjusted, I saw that the person behind the wheel was waving me through, wanting me to cross first. Confused, I shrugged and quickly rushed to the other side. Only when I was safely on the sidewalk did he proceed. I had never heard of such a thing in all my life!

The others were laughing at me. Bastards. "This is not Ratlam," JD chided. "This is the US of A…pedestrians have the right of way here, rookie."

Everything JD said I took with a grain of salt. He was from Ahmedabad, so his behavior was expected. But Satya? He was supposed to be my ally. "Why are *you* laughing, asshole? Do you even have a single four-wheeled vehicle in your clunky little Jangaon?"

"Now that you mention it, no. No we do not. But you sure have 'em in Ratlam. You should at least know how to cross a road, rookie!" And he laughed some more.

I wasn't in the mood to be teased. I probably wouldn't be able to eat for days, I'd have no furniture for months, and my budget buddy was now turning against me. I decided to take the high road and confess my culture shock.

"Bros, I am shocked. I have never been greeted with so much honor – ever – in my entire life. I have never let a pedestrian cross in front of my flying Pulsar, and I certainly wouldn't have dared to assume the right of way as a pedestrian. I'm…flabbergasted."

"Flabbergasted?" JD repeated. "Where'd you learn English, a British nunnery?" He raised his voice three octaves and put on his best-worst British accent. "Oh, dear! You've just caught a glimpse of my *nekkid* arm and now I'm flabbergasted!"

They all laughed and continued to make fun of my choice of words. At least they stopped making fun of the way I crossed the street. That, somehow, was more humiliating. I loved the word flabbergasted and I'm sure I picked it up from an American movie, so I didn't really care what they had to say about it. They were obviously jealous that I spoke better English than they did.

14

TODAY'S PAIN TOMORROW'S GAIN

I was shocked to find out, upon receiving my schedule for the semester, that I had only three lectures (at three hours each) per week. That was a total of nine hours a week. In engineering school, I sat through nine hours of lecture *per day*, so this was a welcomed, albeit surprising change. I wasn't really sure what to expect.

My first scheduled lecture was *The Basic Concepts of Marketing*, taught by Steven McDaniel on Mondays from 6 to 9 PM. JD, Natasha and Shalini had enrolled for the same course, so we decided to go together. My terrible habit of always running late hadn't changed, however, and they left without me. After frantically locating the class, I finally arrived at 6:10 PM, panting and looking like an idiot. I waited at the door, trying to assess the situation. In India, if you were late you had to stand at the door with your tail between your legs and politely beg for admittance. I let my breath regulate itself, and then I said a little too softly, "May I come in, sir?" Though, the professor ignored me. I perused the crowd and saw that a girl was waving me in.

I took her cue, and entered the room. I chose a seat in the last row, my all-time favorite location.

I found out later that, sure, professors dislike late-comers because they disturb the mood of the class and disrupt the flow, but people snuck in late all the time. You don't need permission to enter. That was probably a good thing, knowing me.

Professor McDaniel seemed extraordinarily well-versed in his field but his accent was a little difficult for me to decipher. As I was getting used to his inflections, I lowered my eyes and caught a glimpse of the silkiest blond hair I think I've ever seen. Sitting in front of me was the girl attached to the aforementioned hair. I was mesmerized. My trance was shattered as the professor announced that we were to get into groups of four. *In the middle of a class?* I thought. *That's strange…*

Compelled to follow his instruction, me and the three others sitting next to each other formed a group: the blonde Katie Sterling, my first international friend Fu, an African friend Blake, and I.

After our introductions, Professor Steven piped in with some instructions. "Discuss the various channels of marketing and two applications of each."

Isn't it YOUR job to explain these things? I thought. In India we were never given free rein of a conversation in the classroom. This was new to me, but I think I liked it. And the discussion began.

We were completely engrossed in the discussion as if we were asked to build a marketing strategy for an MNC.

Fu took notes as we kept the discussion going, trying to come with more innovative marketing ideas. The discussion went on for twenty long minutes and we were exhausted afterward. By the end, though, I felt confident about understanding their words. The accents seemed to fade away ever-so-slightly, which was a relief, but my brain was exhausted from participating in the brainstorming session. I had never been required to use that much brain power in a lecture before. Back then, the lecturer spoon-fed us the answers and all that was required was our physical presence. No one cared if our minds were somewhere else. Here, though, we were asked to participate. I wasn't sure whether to be happy or annoyed. This would definitely help me improve my communication skills, which should certainly be an inherent part of any education.

At the end of the discussion, Professor Steven asked each group to make a small presentation on the key points. *C'mon. This is ridiculous!* I thought to myself as my heart started racing. Never had I ever had to get up and make a presentation in a lecture class, and certainly not with such short notice. Now I was annoyed. Definitely not happy!

The first and second groups took turns presenting their brainstormed ideas. They did well, but unfortunately for us they had some of the same ideas we had. Our challenge was to present the same points with a different style, so we jumped up and went third. Katie started the presentation, thankfully, as she was originally from the US and had an excellent command of the English language. I went second. I used every tool I'd ever learned, and I still stumbled. I began filling the gaps with *umms* and likes and *you-know-what-I-means*. I decided to quit when I felt I was ahead and passed the buck to Fu. She was nervous, but she did her best to articulate the talking points, and did well. Blake spoke casually and used his sense of humor to engage the crowd. It was as if he was talking to a group of friends. I made a mental note to remember that tactic in the future.

When all the groups were done their presentations, Professor Steven came up to the podium and reviewed each group. It was then that I understood: this was a *sandwich lecture.* The lectures were the bread and our group discussion and presentations were the peanut butter and jelly. As he reviewed our presentations, he added his own comments and expanded on our ideas. Unlike in engineering school, I found here that there was no space during the lecture to zone out or relax. The active participation in those three short hours was far more exhausting than the eight hours a day of passive listening I was used to in India.

To add salt to injury, he gave us homework. We actually had to prepare something for next week, and he informed us that the class would be conducted in the same fashion. Another sandwich lecture. My brain was going to get quite a workout at this school.

After class, the four of us exchanged email IDs so we could be in touch about our assignment. I made sure to double-check Katie's email before excusing myself to find the rest of my Indian team. When I located them, I felt a quick sense of relief with the knowledge that I would be able to slip back into Hindi if I got stuck in English.

"Steven talks so fast!" JD said, as we made our way home. "I couldn't understand half of what he said…"

I felt another twinge of relief. At least I wasn't alone in this. "You couldn't understand *his* English," I said, knowing self-deprecation would be appreciated by this crowd. "I couldn't understand my own! I don't know what kind of crap came out of my mouth in that classroom."

JD shot me a serious look and said, "Yeah, nobody knows what kind of crap came out of your mouth," and he started laughing. *Loudly.*

"Shut up, jack ass…I didn't see anyone clapping for you, either."

"Please stop it, you guys," Shalini interjected. "It was a good enough performance from all of us. We will improve it each week." She said it so sweetly and sensibly we simply couldn't argue.

I crashed when I got home. I felt a sense of satisfaction as I fell asleep. When you sit in a lecture and just listen, passively, you may miss a lot of key points. You may listen without actually understanding. But when you're asked to do a presentation in front of your peers, you must have a basic understanding of the material before you open your mouth. My tendency to shirk work and preparation would not be possible here. Getting a bad grade on a written exam is one thing. Looking like a fool in front of a room full of your peers and potential collaborators is quite another.

15

1$ = 50Rs: THE COST OF LIVING

When it comes to being a student in the USA, tuition is most certainly at the top of the expenditure list. Next comes the living expenses. rent, food, furniture, toiletries, utilities, school supplies, phones (and phone bills), Internet, and many other things that I wasn't even aware of yet. Since we traded phones and computers for eating out and buying furniture, we needed to get some groceries in the house soon. JD asked me to ping Ron to ask about the supermarket he'd mentioned at the GISA meet-up. Coincidentally, he and his roommates were planning to do their shopping that very day, and invited us to join them. So JD, Satya and I met them at their place.

"How far away is it? Are we going by train?" I asked.

"No, by car," Sid answered.

"Ooooh, the same Camry?" I asked in excitement!

"No, we rented one for a few hours…just as we did when we picked you up from the airport." Oh… fancier! I didn't know.

I was floored by the concept of renting a car, especially for such a short amount of time. I used to rent a bicycle by the hour when I was a kid, but a car by the hour? Strange! We reached the car, which was parked a couple of blocks away from their apartment. Ron approached the driver's side and tapped his wallet on the windshield. The doors unlocked. "Wow, this is like *Fast and Furious!*" I said, content to come across yet another cause for culture shock. With an ATM-like card that you keep in your wallet, you can unlock – and drive away in – a car of your choice. And the keys? They were attached to the dashboard. This would never work in India. The company would have to buy new cars every day because no one would ever return them on time, if they returned them at all. Ron drove like an expert and we reached *Bailey's* supermarket in no time. After we'd all gotten out of the car, Ron tapped his wallet again, and the doors locked behind us. This whole thing was amazing to me.

Inside the supermarket, converting dollars into rupees happened naturally, without much conscious thought. I picked up a toothbrush with a price tag that said $4. I quickly calculated the cost in rupees (at that point it was a dollar per 50 rupees) making the toothbrush... Rs. 200! *Are you kidding me? I could buy a year's supply of toothbrushes in India for that.* Next was a bar of soap for a Rs. 100. *Holy crap! I could get four soaps in India for that price.* But I didn't want to be Stinky Pete, so into my cart it went.

And then I got to the actual food. A loaf of bread was $2.50. My stomach lurched as I thought, *Rs.125 was my MONTHLY budget for bread back home.* As much as I hate to admit it, I missed my mother. As much as I teased her for those endless mounds of homemade food she forced upon us, I realized then that I didn't know how good I had it.

I continued to walk through the supermarket, cringing at each new item and its royal price tag. The hellish complication of converting liters to gallons and grams to ounces seemed like nothing compared to the sticker shock I was experiencing with each new aisle.

I remembered an arbitrary, yet completely functional and frighteningly accurate, conversion rate called *'factor 20,' which illustrates how much a similar item would cost in India.* For example: if a T-shirt costs $15 in the US, multiply the cost by twenty, which equals Rs. 300. So spending $15 on that t-shirt in the US would give you the same kick as buying the same T-shirt for Rs. 300 in India. Similarly, buying a car worth $10,000 in the US would give you the same pinch as buying that same car for Rs. 200,000 in India. And buying a $1 pen in the US would feel the same as buying the same pen for Rs. 20, and so on. This calculation just goes to show it is twenty times more painful to spend in dollars when you earn in rupees.

With a full cart and a nervous pang in my stomach, we walked up to the checkout counter. There was no one there. I looked around for an employee, but none of them would make eye contact with me. Sid noticed my confusion and said, "Dude, it's self-check out. We don't need to call anyone over!" He placed the items in front of the sensor one at a time, and with each new item, the machine beeped and displayed the price on the screen. After the last item, the machine asked him to swipe a credit card. And that was it! Easy breezy. Sid paid for this round, and we'd figure out how much the rest of us owed him once we got home.

There are certain items one cannot get at your general grocery store. We Indians have needs that can only be fulfilled at Indian stores. Luckily, there was one such store not too far from campus! As soon as we entered the market, I was rejuvenated. All the smells of home swished around me as memories of childhood started flipping, like a photo album, through my mind. My family need not worry about me anymore…I had found all the necessities of home. To name a few: Evergreen Parle G biscuits, Royal Basmati rice, Blue Bottle Parachute oil, every spice you could ever hope for, and the list could go on. The item that surprised me the most was in the second aisle I wandered into. My heart jumped as my eyes fell upon the packet of *Ratlami Sev!* I was so pleased, I wanted to grab all of the packets and hug them tightly to my chest. I felt a real sense of pride seeing my birthplace on those packets, and my beaming smile stayed for the rest of the day, despite the price of things.

As I grabbed frozen ready-to-eat *naan* and curries, I noticed JD impatiently roaming the store with a frustrated look on his face. "What the hell are you looking for?" I asked, without an ounce of compassion.

"Chicken. My chicken," he said. I'd never seen him look so worried. Was this chicken a long-lost sibling? I was about to make fun of him further when Satya came bounding through with his cart. JD eyed the giant bag of rice and three large boxes of yogurt.

"Dude, are you planning to sell these in Harbor Point or something?"

"No," Satya smiled, knowing we'd think he was strange. "I eat rice and yogurt for breakfast every day. This'll barely last a week."

Sid came over with a bag of chicken and handed it to JD. His expression immediately changed to that of a puppy that had just been given a giant bone. I was anxious because those poor chickens were going to be cooked in our shared oven.

A LABORERS JOB? GOD NO!

After our shopping spree, we sorted out the groceries at Ron's apartment. I saw the receipts and nearly had a heart attack.

"$262 for a few groceries?" I gasped. "That's 13,000 Rupees!"

"Don't worry." Ron laughed, "you will earn it all back. Hey speaking of which, how's the job search going?"

We looked at each other with blank expressions on our faces. None of us had even started.

"I'm not sure where to start!" I said, as I sifted through our purchases.

"There are two good departments to work for," said Sid. We three stood still for a second just like a soldier in attention stance.

"Parking and food court," Sid disclosed.

"I'm serious!" I said, chuckling at what I wanted to be joke. Being an engineer, I didn't want to believe that those were my options.

"I'm serious too," he replied, not understanding how I thought it was a joke.

"And what would I do there? Any IT-related work?" I said, wishing it to be true.

"No," Sid said bluntly. "At the parking lot you'd have to monitor cars and collect cash."

"And what about the food court?" JD asked. I could tell he was anxious too.

"Cook in the kitchen, serve at the counter, or work as a cashier!" Ron answered.

"We came to the US to earn a global MBA, not to monitor cars and serve food. NO WAY will I take —"

"Okay," I interrupted, trying to defuse the situation. "Out of curiosity, why do you consider those good jobs?"

Ron looked at us patiently. He understood our agitation and explained, "Listen, we know where you're coming from. You've paid your dues in India, you've worked in corporates and your families are successful and this feels like a giant step down. But you're not in India anymore. You're in a new country where you have to start at the bottom to get to the top. We all took menial jobs and went through this phase and, believe it or not, it's been one of the most rewarding phases of our college existence thus far. Would you agree, Sid?"

"Absolutely. I agree, one hundred percent."

Ron continued: "First of all, who the hell cares what you do in the US? No one here is judging you. Secondly, your part-time job would pay nearly forty thousand rupees a month. Think about it. You wouldn't need to call home and ask for money, and you wouldn't have to stress over the little things. Every experience here is a learning experience, and even the most mundane job is way more valuable than sitting idly at home. The best part is, you make new friends and gain exposure. That's priceless."

JD bounced from the couch and asked: "How do we apply?"

Ron's speech seemed to have convinced us all, and we stood at attention as he answered. "Ask for Scott in the parking department, and Tony Philips in the food court."

We returned home and each secretly got very serious about the job search. Of course, we acted as if we didn't care, because who in their right mind would want to drum up more competition by showing their excitement? I had the bright idea to wake up early the next morning and be the first one to meet Scott and Tony. When I walked into the kitchen at the crack of dawn, however, I saw JD eating breakfast… Or, more accurately, stuffing his mouth like a starved pig. I looked down and saw that he was wearing a shiny pair of dress shoes. Great minds think alike, I suppose.

"What are you up to so early in the morning?" I asked.

His demeanor changed as soon as he saw me. He slowed down his eating and leaned back with a relaxed, *hakuna matata* expression and said, "Nothing much, bro. I have to hand over some documents to the management office, that's all." But before I could get another word out, he was gone. And he left the door open, too. I scanned the apartment to see what my other roommates were up to. Satya was in the shower and Khanna was still snoring in his bed. I got ready as quickly as I could. By the time I was done, Satya was also about to leave the house.

"What are you up to so early in the morning?" I asked him, trying to assess the situation.

With a slight tremble in his voice he said, "Nothing man, just going to see a professor for course info."

Huh? Either he was really nervous about meeting with a professor, or he was lying. I wondered if these two were up to the same shenanigans I was up to.

Sure enough, as I reached Scott's office I saw that Satya was already waiting outside. Going to see his professor, my ass. He smiled when he saw me, but his eyes betrayed him. I could see the shame behind the coy veneer.

"So you're taking the parking course this semester?" I teased.

"I just thought I'd…ummmm…"

"It's okay," I said, interrupting whatever bogus excuse he was about to come up with. We had a common goal, and we both chose to conceal it from each other. I couldn't blame him for lying about where he was going…In fact, I should've known not to even ask in the first place. The days of completing assignments collectively were over. This wasn't engineering school. This was real life.

We both had to wait in the reception area, because Scott was interviewing another candidate. I thought back to how quickly JD skedaddled after I asked him what he was up to. I was willing to bet a million dollars he was in that room, but I didn't dare say it out loud lest my suspicions were wrong. I absolutely should've made that bet. Ah yes, another liar amongst us. The three of us just laughed when JD emerged from Scott's office. We were the perfect triumvirate: *Sindhi* who can't stand to lose a penny, *Baniya* who can't stand to spend a penny, and *Gulti* who can't stand to miss an opportunity to make a penny.

Satya, having arrived ever-so-slightly earlier than I did, went first. JD and I were left facing each other in the waiting area.

"Where are you off to now?" I asked.

"Do you have to ask?"

"Nope. See you there!"

While Satya was in his interview and I was alone in the waiting area, I found myself praying to God. I prayed so hard, it was as if I had come to the United States to become a parking attendant. I was in the middle of repeating the prayer (it couldn't hurt) when Satya emerged from Scott's office. It was my turn. I tucked in my shirt and checked my hair before going in – something I had never even thought to do back home – and walked into the office with as much confidence as any parking attendant should have. Scott stood up to greet me and it was like saying hello to the Eiffel Tower. He was 6'5" and muscular. Not just muscular, built… like he worked hard to get that way. I decided right then and there to always stay on his good side.

"Hi Scott, I am Kartik," I said with a giant smile. I really wanted this job.

"Hey *Khautik*, nice to meet you." He motioned for me to sit down. "What can I do for you?"

"I'm looking for a part-time job," I said, not letting go of that smile.

"Okay. Just fill out this form and I'll let you know." And with that, he turned to his computer and started rat-a-tat-tatting on his keyboard.

I began filling out the form, wishing there was more of an interview and not just the mundane paperwork. As I tried to remember my new address in order to write it on the form, I flashed on a memory of flattering my engineering professors before the practical exam.

"Hey Scott," I said, not really knowing what I would say next.

"Yes?" He looked up from the computer so I had to come up with something fast.

"I've heard a lot about you… I mean, people told me the parking lot is really the best place to work around here. They said that working with you is like taking a management course."

"Really?" He asked with a broad, pearly-white smile. "You heard that from people?"

"I did." I said confidently.

Eager to prove me right, he started talking about his experiences. I listened intently, trying only to ensure that he remembers my face when it came to hiring. There were more than fifty applications for only five positions and I had to stand out somehow. Getting him to talk about himself, connecting to him on a personal level, was something I'd learned during that first marketing lecture. *Selling is not about what the seller wants to say, but rather what the client wants to hear.* I was trying to sell myself, so I made him feel good about himself. Genius.

"Thanks for your time, Scott. Let me know if you need me!"

"Sure," he said casually, and went back to his computer as if we'd never had that little chat. I half-expected him to hire me right there on the spot, but apparently that wasn't in the cards. I was dismayed. I couldn't tell if he was going to hire me or not, and I just wanted to know.

My next destination was to see Tony Philips, the manager at the food court. I entered his office and tried to apply the same adulation technique, but this time it failed. He was extremely busy, and didn't have time for flattery, so I quietly filled out my application and left. I hit up various other departments on my way out. Wherever I saw an open door, I scooted in to see if they were hiring. It was a long day.

16

WHAT MAKES YOU HAPPIER – LUXURY OR TOGETHERNESS?

Two full weeks of my new life had passed. I came up for air in my new ocean with all the new fish, and realized my life was going much faster than ever before. Everything was different, and life was a whirlwind. Meals were eaten on-the-go and as quickly as possible. Rupees had become dollars, Nokia had become Apple, friends were new and, most importantly, family was non-existent. I wasn't just living in a different city. I was in a new country on other side of the globe – an independent journey.

I'd had fun meeting new people these past couple weeks, but when I stopped to assess, I found the person I was missing most from back home was Sonia. We agreed to Skype, so early Saturday morning (which was Friday, late evening, in India), I logged in to Skype without so much as brushing my teeth or running a comb through my hair. The screen was dark for some time and, for a moment I thought she'd forgotten that we had scheduled this time to talk. I felt a knot forming in my stomach. It had been two weeks since we'd seen each other, how could she forget me so soon? As I was beginning to wallow in my self-pity, a burst of light came across the screen and all those familiar blip-blooping Skype sounds came through my earplugs. Sonia appeared on the screen and I couldn't believe what I saw: She wore my favorite red dress – which I always asked her to wear out on our special dates – and her hair was wet with curls, just the way I liked it. She wore the little heart-shaped earrings I had given her for Valentine's day, and in the gleam of the candle light she looked like a beautiful angel. She closed her eyes and put a red rose in front of the camera. I was speechless. When she raised her eyes and looked right into the camera, I could see that they were filled with tears. I felt the emotion bubble up inside me, replacing the pity knot with one of unexpected sorrow. And also butterflies, the very same ones that giddy puppy love is made of.

"I just love you," I said breathlessly. I swallowed hard to fight the tears I could feel clumping in my throat. I was completely taken aback by these emotions. Where was this coming from?

She smiled and said nothing. "You are the most beautiful angel. How are you, baby?"

Sonia shrugged and didn't say a word. I had a feeling she was holding back so many tears that she couldn't find her voice.

"How was your day? Tell me a little bit about what's going on for you!" I thought I'd take the focus off of us, and our relationship and how sad it was that we weren't together, and make it more about how well things were going individually. I thought that might take the angst out of the conversation.

Sonia took a breath for what seemed like the first time since we got on this face-to-face call. I think it worked. She found her voice. "My day was good!" She said with a light-hearted air about her. "I have good news…"

"How exciting. What is it?" I asked eagerly.

"First, give me my chocolates," she said with a mischievous smile. A joke! That was a step in the right direction.

"I will buy you a factory, just please tell me your news!"

She waited a bit, letting the suspense build a little more. Finally she said, "I got a job."

"Wow. That's wonderful! Where? Doing what?"

"In Raghu's office. He has really tried hard for me to get job in legal department for a CA position."

"Oh nice! Congratulations…But Raghu never…??" I was happy at the same time disturbed with the fact why Raghu never told me about this.

"It was so nice of him. I owe him a big treat." She smiled.

"Hmm…When do you have to start?" I tried to hide my intuitiveness.

"This Monday."

"We should celebrate!"

She went silent. "Soni, you okay?" I asked, after letting the silence linger for a moment.

"Karti, I missed you a lot today. I got my first job and all I wanted was to celebrate with you. But you were…"

"Hey *baccha*, I am with you always. We will celebrate now. I'll be right back."

I went to the kitchen for a coke and few chocolates we'd just gotten from the grocery store. I sat back down at my computer and held them up to the camera. "Flowers, chocolates, a little beverage, and the two of us. What else do we need in this world?" I asked playfully.

"I wish you could hold me, Karti."

"Close your eyes and I will."

She let her lids flutter shut as I talked her through all of the sensations of being held. We imagined being in each other's arms, and it was nice for a moment, but I felt something missing. Something beyond words.

SHARING HAPPINESS

After the call with Sonia I was back to my life in the New World. I spent the rest of the day involved in arranging household stuff with my roommates. That night, we crashed early, having expended so much energy on getting our house set up. The next morning, I woke up to an iPhone on one side of me, and a MacBook on the other on my bed-cum-chair beanbag. It reminded me of when I was a kid and I'd fall asleep with my new toys clutched to my chest. I'd wake up in the morning with a delightful pain in my back, having rolled over and slept on my new yellow Tonka truck (or some such thing) all night.

I decided I needed to share my new happiness and what better tool did I have than the newly-popular

Facebook? I updated my profile with a Bollywood-style photo: Me in my new apartment holding an iPhone in one hand and a MacBook in the other. I had a smarmy, self-important look on my face, as if I'd just signed a million-dollar deal. I added the caption: 'King of the Apple World.' I got more than fifty likes. In those days, fifty likes was a big deal.

I also got several comments:

Meenal wrote: *From Nokia to Apple...nicee KJ* ☺.

One of my friends from high school wrote: *Oh Kool Americano!* True enough.

Proud of you. Love <3. That one was from Sonia. Cute that she posted, even though I'd already shared my new toys with her. It felt supportive to have her comment alongside my other buddies. But I was especially delighted to see my engineering roomies chime in.

Kabeer wrote: *Bhai dhool saaf kar liya karna kabhi kabhi (Bro, try to clean the dust occasionally):* p...He knew me well... Indeed, I was not known for my dusting capabilities.

Raghu: *Great job bhai. Happy for you* ☺

One of my other high school friends asked if they were authentic, or if I had just pasted Apple stickers on knock-offs. Totally something I would do.

When I got to the next comment my stomach jumped a little. *"Angelina's effect ;)"* Satya had written. I hoped Sonia wouldn't see that, or at least wouldn't ask questions about it, true as it was.

Other friends joked on the fact that I'd gone from a poor bastard who only put one liter of gas in his motorcycle at a time and let her run on fumes, to a guy living the life with two fancy Apple gadgets.

I was so happy. It made me feel, for those few moments, that I was connected to my old life, and that those people were still just a stone's throw away.

ARE YOU WITH ME OR AGAINST ME?

The third week of my new life was underway, and appeared to be a regular week with the usual preparations for class presentations and assignments. Not to mention the continued job search. I made the rounds again, making stops at the parking lot, food court, library, IT lab, media lab, and even a few new places I hadn't hit before. I learned in my new fancy marketing class that, image repetition is key. The more someone sees something, the more likely they are to think of it when they have a need for it. So I showed my face as often as possible.

One evening, Khanna, JD, and I were sitting in the living room, each doing our homework. Satya had just come from the university and entered the apartment, took a deep breath, and fell dramatically onto the couch. "Guys…" he said, with an expectant tone.

We looked up to see if there was more. He didn't say another word, so we went back to doing our own thing.

"Guys…" He said again, wanting us to goad him on. When he saw that we weren't taking the bait, he let out a frustrated grunt and said, "Guys…I got a job."

"Damn, really?" JD said, unable to hide his jealousy.

"Oh man!" I said, feeling happy for him but at the same time wondering why they'd chosen him over me despite all my best efforts.

"Shooooot, are you kidding me?" Khanna didn't even try to hide his disdain. "Where? How?"

"In the IT lab," Satya answered, downplaying how proud of himself he was in an attempt to allay our feelings of contempt and jealousy. JD didn't catch on to this subtlety, though.

"Fuck you man," JD said, "What'll you do there?"

"I'll work as a lab supervisor, I guess."

Trying to be the supportive one, I said, "Woohoo! Congratulations, man. We should celebrate." I looked over at JD at one point, and he looked like he had just received terrible news – like his favorite pet had just died or something. He was definitely not in a celebratory mood. Who could blame him? It was a mere side effect of friendly competition.

I sulked silently for about a week. I had a little less fervor in my job search and I actually felt betrayed. I had worked so hard but hadn't gotten a single offer. One morning I was sitting at my laptop, puttering around the web when a new email popped up. I jumped two feet in the air, and when I came back down, I clicked on the it. It was from Scott Adams, the very first interview I had.

"Dear Mr. Jain, Congratulations. Your résumé matched our profile. We would like to hire you. If you are interested, please visit our office for further details."

It wasn't fancy, but it was a job offer! Within a minute, I was in Scott's office, so excited you'd have thought I had just landed my first full-time dream job after receiving my MBA. Scott called me in. "Hi again. *Khautik* right?"

He could call me anything he wanted. He was giving me a job. "Yeah. *Khautik*," I said with a smile.

"Are you interested in working with us, then?"

"Absolutely."

"Cool. This is James Manning…but you can call him Jimmy." Jimmy came over begrudgingly. "Jimmy, this is *Khautik* – your new colleague. He will be working with you in lot C."

"What will I be doing there?" I asked abruptly.

"You gotta open the gate for visitors, and collect the cash," said Scott.

Oh fuck man, NO WAY! I remembered our cashier, *Lalaram*, who used to work at our wholesale grocery shop in Ratlam. He would leave his post to open the gate whenever my dad wanted to park his prized possession – essentially his third child – *Maruti-800*. My dad would mock him and call him by his nick name, *Lalu*, which was a bit derogatory. I used to mock him, too. And now I was beneath him. At least he had been working at a retail shop. Far more classy than a parking lot.

Jimmy asked me to follow him. He was a tall, gangly, blond kid with long uncombed hair and a careless (not to be confused with carefree) way about him. He wore a thick plaid hoody, which looked like it hadn't been washed for several years. His jeans were nested below his butt cheeks, and I could clearly see *Hanes* written in bold on the waistband of his underwear. Classy, indeed.

"How long have you been working here?" I asked.

He scratched his head and replied: "Umm…somewhere around a year. A little more than a year now, I guess."

We reached the lot, which was a five-minute walk from the office. It was a giant square that could hold up to five hundred cars at a time. He led me to the ramshackle booth, which was located at the entrance of the parking lot, and was attached to a very noisy gate. In the booth, there was a small sliding window, from which you would reach out and collect the cash. A small space heater was set up in the corner, to help you survive Boston's potentially fatal winters. I had mixed feelings about this job. It would certainly pay the bills but, at the same time, I didn't want to be someone else's *Lalu*. In the end, though, it would be an experience – one that I would never have gotten in India – so I accepted.

Jimmy introduced me to the guy in the booth. "This is Terrell. He's also my roommate."

"Nice to meet you, bro. Welcome." He then looked around to make sure no one else was in earshot. He winked at me and asked, "You smoke?"

"No. Ummm…I mean, ummmm…"

"C'mon dude!" Saved by Jimmy. "It's his first day. Let him at least settle down." I didn't know why that was such a difficult question to answer. I felt pressured somehow, like I had to say the right thing to fit in with this crowd or something.

Jimmy changed the subject and began explaining the job. "When cars come in, you gotta press the button to open the gate. When they leave, you have to collect $5."

"Okay," I said. "Sounds good…" and we began walking back towards the office. Was that the extent of my training? It seemed like it would be the easiest job in the world.

"Where do you live?" Jimmy asked, trying to fill the silence.

"Harbor Point,"

"Cool. That's where we live too. Which building?"

"We live in 35."

"Really? We live in 40, right next to you. Stop by anytime."

"Yeah sure," I said, not really knowing if he was friend material.

"Great. See you tomorrow!" And with that, he was gone.

On the way back to home, I was feeling pretty good about myself. Classes were going well, I got a new job…I was pumped to share with the good news with friends and family. The first person I called was my dad, expecting him to be surprised and delighted to know that his son got a job. As soon as he picked the phone, I said, "Dad, good news."

"What, *bete*?"

"Dad, I got a part-time job!" I said in a high-spirited tone.

"Oh, excellent. Where?" He seemed excited.

"The parking lot," I said in a proud booming voice.

"WHAT?"

"The parking lot, Dad," I repeated.

"What do you have to do there?" His tone was lowered down.

"I have to open the gate and collect cash," I tried to keep my spirits high, even though I could feel his utter disappointment.

And then there was complete silence. I thought for a moment that the phone was disconnected. "Dad? Are you there?"

"Okay, tell me how is your new home? Did you settle down?" He changed the subject, as was his way when something did not sit well with him. Don't address it, God forbid, just talk about something else.

"I moved in with Jatin, Satya and Mohit. We are settling in quite nicely."

"Are they vegetarians?" His tone was that of an investigator, trying to get to the bottom of a vile murder.

Just as the image of JD scaling the walls of the Indian store for his damn chicken came to mind, I said, "Yeah dad, they're vegetarian." I lied because lying was easier than answering his follow-up questions. *"How do you cook?" "Do you use the same dishes?"etc.* Moreover, I didn't want to make him, or my mom, uncomfortable.

"Oh very nice, *bete.*" To him, vegetarian roommates was more of an achievement than getting a job that would pay my bills. So typical! He continued to ask the same monotonous questions he'd been asking since childhood.

I told him about my classes, some of the culture shock I was experiencing, and about some of my favorite professors.

"Great. Just remember, you have gone there to study, and study only. Do as much hard work as you can. Your future depends on these two years."

"Sure, Dad." My stock answer for all of his serious moments.

"How are Mom and Aditi?" I asked, hoping he'd hand the phone over to one of them.

"Your mom has gone to temple and Aditi has already left for school. I will ask them to call you when they get back."

We said our goodbyes, and I headed into the common areas of the apartment, looking to share my news with my roommates.

JD was in the kitchen. Excellent. I wanted to share this news, yes, but let me be honest: I wanted to make him jealous.

"I have news for you," I said.

"What?" he asked as he dished curry onto his plate.

"Guess."

"I don't play guessing games when I'm hungry. Just tell me."

"I got a job," I said, raising my eyebrows in a boasting fashion.

"Really?" He started coughing, choking on the forkful of curry he'd just shoveled into his mouth. "Wow, man, congrats. Where?"

"Parking."

"Oh, you're Scott's boy."

I happily grabbed a plate for dinner, knowing I'd one-upped him. "I also have news," he said as I put the first bite up to my lips.

"Oh, yeah?"

"I also got a job."

"Really? Where?"

"Food court."

"Oh, so you're Tony's boy. Nice!" I said. "You should really wash my dishes from now. You have to practice, you know?"

"Shut up, parking cheapskate." I wasn't quite sure what he meant by that. I'm sure he was trying to offend me!

THE FIRST DAY OF LABOR

My first day on the job, I was running ten minutes late, as usual, and I rushed into the booth as soon as I arrived. Jimmy and Terrell were already there, waiting, but they didn't say anything about my tardiness. Terrell simply asked me to take his place so he could go outside and monitor the cars. On the desk, there was a stack of dollar bills and a whole lot of coins: half-dollars, quarters, dimes, nickels and pennies. I hadn't dealt with a lot of change yet, so I was wicked confused. Haha! *Wicked.* I was catching on to the Boston slang. Everything was wicked. Good and bad. I was beginning to really like that word. Anyway, Jimmy helped me figure out the coin situation. "You don't see a lot of these," he said, as he held up a half-dollar coin. I was about to respond, when a car pulled up.

"Good morning!" said the gorgeous girl behind the wheel. She handed over $5 and I opened the gate, smiling politely and perhaps a bit flirtatiously. "Thanks!" she said with a sweet smile. Then she was off.

The next twenty drivers that came through thanked me as I took their money and I opened the gate for them. There was something wrong with this picture. This much politeness and even, I'd go so far as to say, respect for a parking attendant? I couldn't help but feel flattered. I looked back in time and remembered all the gate-keepers from my high school and college. Not only had I never said 'thank you,' I never even acknowledged their existence. Anyhow, in the present, I happily opened the gate for four hours straight, without getting tired. Who, I ask you, would get tired of hundreds of people (including some hot girls) giving you sweet smiles, so early in the morning?

My shift was over at noon, and I realized I was wicked hungry. I went to the food court, hoping that I might see JD. I was curious to see how he was doing. I arrived, and after I caught my first glimpse of him, I couldn't stop laughing. He had a tall white chef's hat on his head, and was serving burgers. Though I didn't eat burgers, I stood in line so I could fuck with him. When I got to the front of the line, I acted as if I'd never met him before. I ordered from him in a mean, bossy tone: "Hey! Gimme a burger… and be quick about it."

"Bhencho…" As he was about to talk back to me, in an equally abusive tone, he realized Tony Philip was standing next to him. Unable to respond, he served my burger with a smile.

"Thanks, garcon!" I said, and smiled at Tony as I passed him. I was laughing my ass off at this *Gujju-Sindhi*, who had a reputable business in India, flipping burgers in the US. I intentionally grabbed a table right in front, where he couldn't help but see me, and teased him with every bite I took.

After eating, I remembered that I needed to print something out. I headed to the computer lab. Satya was sitting at the reception desk. His job was to make sure students were able to access the computers, and he would troubleshoot should anyone have an issue. I was glad to see him.

The three of us were enjoying our jobs. Different as they were, they each had their own benefits. I started to think this was the best part of life in the US. Every job seemed to be treated equally, with the same dignity and respect, whether it was parking or software engineering. And what's more, it seems people work in certain areas by choice, not because they were forced by their father, or out of fear of breaking a cultural norm.

The next afternoon, when I got home from work, I had a message from Sonia. "Missing you..."

Needing my post-work snack, I grabbed some bread and cheese and then quickly logged on to Skype. It was 10:30 PM in India. Sonia seemed exhausted, and was in her PJs and flowing night-time hair. She smiled, trying to fight the sleepiness that was starting to overcome her. She placed a bouquet of flowers in front of the camera.

"Hey, cutie Wow! You look so beautiful. Where did those flowers come from?"

"From Rahul's gift shop in front of *Shake & Bake*. He was asking about you!"

"Really?"

"Yeah. You used to be one of his best customers! I told him not to worry, that I would buy flowers from him on a regular basis. He wanted me to tell you that you are missed."

"Oh, that Rahul! I'm surprised he thought I was a good customer…I used to pick the flowers for you and run. I never paid him on time!" I held the laptop screen, looked in her eyes and said, "Sonia…"

"Hmm?"

"I just love you."

"Huh," she said indifferently, "I don't."

"So who's this all for, then?" I asked, casually calling her bluff.

"For the person who used to hold me!" she held her silence for a moment, and then whispered, "Life was so beautiful here Karti. Why did you leave?"

"Life is still beautiful, honey. See, we can feel love for each other!" I knew that wasn't the answer she wanted, but it was the only one I had. "What did you have to eat today?" I asked, trying to change the subject.

"Nothing, really. I haven't been that hungry."

"Honey, you have to eat."

"Karti, will you hold me? I just miss you so much."

"Missing you too, *baccha*. Come to me. Don't worry, we will be together soon."

We sat in silence for a while, pretending to hold each other. When I realized she'd fallen asleep, I called her name gently to wake her. I watched as she climbed into bed, and once she was safely nestled in, I shut down my computer.

The next day, work was slow. Jimmy and I 'shot the shit' (another American term I was coming to like very much) all day. It felt as if we'd known each other since childhood. As we talked, I learned more and more about the social and cultural differences between the US and India. At one point, I looked over at him and he had his eyes closed. His eyes had seemed heavy all day. "Hey man, what's up? You seem especially tired today."

"It's nothing, dude. I just didn't sleep last night."

"Why, what happened?" I asked, more worried than curious.

"Fucking Rachael crashed at my place last night. We were up all night, if you know what I mean."

Sure. Sonia and I had those nights. We'd talk till the wee hours of the morning. I put my hands on his shoulders and said in a compassionate tone, "Yeah man, I know how it is. You look terrible, though. Next time you're this tired, let me know and I'll cover for you." I winked at him.

"Haha thanks man, I'll remember that… So, do you have a girlfriend?" asked Jimmy.

"Yes, back in India. We are in a long-distance relationship."

He laughed, "What? How does that work?"

"We talk on the phone, or Skype."

"You're in a relationship and you don't get to bang her?" he seemed utterly unhinged by this notion.

"No, but we're happy," I said, noticing that I was trying to convince myself as much as I was trying to convince him.

"Oh man, I wouldn't be able to do that!" Jimmy said, shaking his head at me. I guess for him, a relationship wasn't a relationship without banging.

"What about you? How did you meet Rachel?"

"We met at a house party at my friends place…last week."

"Just last week and she was at your place? Dude, you work fast! I couldn't touch my girlfriend for months after we started dating!" I had no idea it was even possible to move that quickly in a relationship."

"Really? No wonder your right hand looks so much stronger."

"Shut up, jackass! So…where do your parents live?" I asked, trying to change the subject.

He reached up, mindlessly started playing with his hair, and said, "My dad lives with his girlfriend about an hour from here." I had never heard of such a thing. Those two words: *'Dad's girlfriend'* had never been uttered in the same sentence in India.

"And your mom?" I asked.

"She just moved to Florida with her boyfriend not too long ago."

His mom had a boyfriend, too? This was new territory for me. I was especially surprised at how casually (and willingly) he was sharing this information – as if he were talking about doing laundry.

"So who is paying for your education?" I asked. I didn't want to pry, but I was really curious. And he didn't seem to mind the questions.

"I am. It's kinda' bullshit, but my parents won't pay. I'm just working to save up some money, and I'll start undergrad next year."

"Great!"

"What do you mean, great?" He seemed a little pissed.

"Oh, I just mean it's great that my dad isn't privy to this concept of paying your own way through college," I said. I couldn't help but laugh. I got a little chuckle out of him, too.

"You are one lucky dude…"

"Yes, yes I am."

17

OH, GRINDING! WHAT'S THAT?

Receiving your first paycheck is certainly cause for celebration. After working for a month, we each received our first fifteen-day paycheck – worth more than two months of my full-time salary in India. It was astonishing. Khanna, Natasha and Shalini didn't have to work, as their pocket-money was more than a part-time job pay. Lucky them.

"*Saalo*, you all got jobs, and now you got money too… Where's the party?" Khanna asked with excitement. We took his question very seriously, and after a moment of discussion, we decided to go to clubbing. Some say clubbing in the US is as educational as attending college there. So, why not?

"Let's go tomorrow," Khanna said. "It is a Friday, and as we all know, that's virgin night…" Did we all know that? I wasn't aware of that fact, but I went with it.

We jumped on our laptops and started searching for the hottest clubs in Boston. The first one that showed up was called *The Jaz* and seemed to be the most vibrant of all the ones we looked at, subsequently. It was rated five out of five, and had pictures of sexy girls hanging on guys. *That'll do*, I thought…

My last class on Friday was Basic Finance. I could barely concentrate, because I was day-dreaming about the fun, upcoming. The class finally ended at 8:45 PM, and it was time to get ready to go clubbing.

When I got home, I ironed a new white shirt and a pair of slim trousers, polished my shoes, put deodorant on (and two types of cologne) and placed a tie carefully in my pocket, in case the club required that I wear one. I learned the tie trick from my dad, who told me to keep it handy for seminars and interviews. I got ready quickly (in about the same amount of time it would take me to get ready for engineering college every morning) and met my roommates in the living room. We all were very smartly dressed and looked ready for a night on the town. It almost looked as if we were going to crash a wedding. We looked *that* good.

To get to the club, we had to catch Bus Number 8, which ran between Harbor Point and the nearest subway station. JD showed off a fancy app he'd installed on his iPhone called *Bus Locator*. It indicated that there would be a bus in three minutes and forty-five seconds. Sure enough, exactly three minutes and forty-five seconds later, it pulled over and coughed open its doors. I was amazed at how precise the timing was unlike it was for buses in Indore. In fact, if you were running five or ten minutes late, odds were that you'd still catch it.

By the time we'd transferred from the bus to the train and arrived at the club, it was 10:30 PM. There was a long queue on the street and we took our places at the end of it. The sign for the club seemed magically lit, flashing lights spelling out *The Jaz* sparkled, changing colors every few seconds. We were transfixed. From where I stood, all I could see was a sea of black, white and red clothing. Those seemed to be the colors of the Boston clubbing scene. It was a chilly night, but that didn't stop girls from wearing tiny dresses that covered just enough to keep you guessing. Faces were impeccably made up. Purses matched shoes, and hairstyles in different kinds were on display. While observing them, I remembered the best chapter of my educational life that was *Ratio and Proportions*. The most attractive (and apparently rare) proportions are 36:24:36 I found as I stood in line, that this was where all the perfectly proportioned people went. I found those measurements in abundance here. Legs were smoother than butter, softer than silk and shinier than diamonds. Some girls almost towered over me with their high heels, but most were just right — a little shorter than me, but still perfectly at eye level. I watched JD as his eyes lit up at the sights around us. This was going to be a good night.

"I think I've died and gone to heaven, bro!" JD seemed hypnotized.

"Who needs an MBA when you've got *The Jaz*?" I joked. I think he thought I was serious because he nodded and said, "You got that right, bro!"

At long last, we reached the door where a bouncer was checking IDs. As we'd only been in the US for a few weeks, we had only passports to show him. Primarily used for security checkpoints at the airport, a much better use was discovered this night: security checkpoints at clubs and bars.

My stomach lurched a little when I handed him my passport. I don't know why, but I was nervous he wouldn't let me in. I stood there, silently panicking when he handed the passport back to me and motioned for me to go inside. Phew! It was really dark as we entered, and the music was pounding in my ears. I couldn't even tell what song it was, it was so loud. The only way to communicate with each other was to shout at the top of your lungs, and even then, it was touch and go. The lobby was furnished with contemporary luxury couches, on which people who'd already had a little too much, had crashed. We crossed the lobby and went inside, where a grand dance floor was flashing with laser beams and intense beats. The dance floor was packed with mostly couples in a position I had never seen before. I learned later that it is called *grinding* and, in the US anyway, is quite common. I looked around and marveled at how different this scene was from Indian clubs, where men struggled to impress the girls; tried too hard, in fact, actively dancing face-to-face to prolong their togetherness. Here, the scene was quite the opposite; guys were standing relaxed, while the girls were shaking and grinding. It was exciting for all of us. Passion and romance were in the air…but not for us that night, or, at least, not on the dance floor, at that moment because we were all singles. The only thing left for us to do was to drink. We sidled up to the bar, where we'd get the fuel (and courage) we needed to make our moves and prolong our fun.

"Let's do some shots!" Khanna screamed in excitement. He was the only one who hadn't found a job, yet he was the most charged and excited among us. We didn't want to be buzz-kills (another American word I picked up this week). Satya, JD and I followed suit. I had never done shots before (I preferred Smirnoff) but I was game for anything. New life, new liquor!

Khanna ordered four shots of tequila from a gorgeous bartender who looked like a movie star. Every time she bent over, I couldn't help but stare at the beautiful lines just above her shirt. Collarbones are my weakness. She filled four glasses with something called *El Jimador*, placed a wedge of lime on each glass, and set a saltshaker right in front of me. I could barely feel my face and I hadn't even taken the shot yet! The four of us took hold of our glasses, looked at each other, clinked glasses and downed the tequila in a gulp. I felt as if someone had rubbed a burning match down my esophagus. I hurriedly licked the salt and sucked on the lime, which had a quick, fire-extinguisher-like effect. As we slammed our shot glasses back down on the bar, Khanna screamed, "Another round!" The Bartender Beauty filled four more glasses and I closed my eyes and clenched my fists in anticipation of the second dose of burning match.

After a moment of silence (did their throats burn too?) Satya, holding his head, said, "I'm done guys!"

Khanna shrieked, "C'mon *Andhra*, one more!" and with that, he ordered four more shots.

Within ten minutes, we'd had five shots apiece. I was a tequila-virgin, so I had no idea what the reaction time and after effects would entail. How bad could it be? Those glasses were tiny! A few minutes later, I found myself enjoying myself more than I thought I could. I felt suddenly like something had unlocked my inhibitions. I became more of a natural, relaxed, and nonchalant version of former myself. I had so much energy! I found myself willing to do things I'd never done before. We agreed to go our separate ways so none of us would become the other's cock-blocker.

I turned my attention 180 degrees to the right and then the left to do a recce. Most girls were either hooking up with their boyfriends, or dancing in small groups, mostly with their girlfriends in tow. I started my journey with a slow, sloppy dance step as I looked around, wondering in which direction the magic was waiting. I barely recognized myself with my carefree attitude, as if I was the happiest guy in the club.

Even with my newfound optimism and the extra spring in my step, I had no luck. People were in their own little worlds and no trial let me succeed. I needed courage to approach a girl and convince her to dance with me. Even after five shots of tequila, there was a constant fight between my heart and mind. My mind kept saying, "Let's approach!" and my heart kept replying, "What if she says no?" And also "What about Sonia?!" "My actions had a thin line between the electrifying atmosphere around and a missing part of my life.

My mind won a few times, but to no avail. After several failed attempts, I stood silently in a corner, watching other people be happy. Then, I decided I needed a drink in hand. When you're alone in a club, you should at least *look* like you're having fun. As I approached the bar, a gorgeous, tall girl with pearly-white skin approached and stood beside me, waiting to order her drink. My hands started tingling, as did other parts of me. Without even thinking, that cliché come-on line came out of my mouth. "May I buy you a drink?" I asked, and immediately, regretted it. I think I was slurring a little. She looked at me with indifference, thought for a second, shrugged and said with a smile, "Sure!" *I love you too*, I thought. Man, she was beautiful! I knew I couldn't really afford it, but after five shots of tequila, I had forgotten that I only made $10 an hour and was living on frozen food…In that moment, the only thing I cared about was making a good impression on this gorgeous girl.

She ordered a *Sex on the Beach*. I wished she'd ordered a cheap beer, but I couldn't exactly rescind my offer. I tried to meet her standards by ordering a Jack and Coke. (It was the only luxury drink I could think of.) The bartender prepared the drinks and placed the check in front of me. I gasped when I saw the price, but covered it well by letting out a little cough. TWENTY-FOUR DOLLARS FOR TWO DRINKS! I immediately sobered up and felt no remnants of the tequila as I furnished my credit card with a huge smile, like it was nothing.

Feeling the rising angst of having just spent almost three hours' salary on drinks, I pushed myself to be brave and ignite some casual banter with my new tall lady friend. Within just a few minutes, it felt as if we'd been friends for life, and I suddenly felt comfortable asking her to hit the dance floor with me. I opened my mouth to say the words, but was stopped dead in my tracks. An African-American guy came out of nowhere and kissed her. And she kissed him back. My eyes widened and I felt as if someone had just kicked me square in the balls. She got up and said, "Hey thanks for the drink, see ya around!" I sat there, wide-eyed and open-mouthed. I wanted to yell, *"Fuck you bitch!"* But that would have been inappropriate. Plus, her boyfriend was a big bulky guy who could've kicked my ass for so much as thinking it. I was left with no option but to fake a smile and wave goodbye. When they were out of sight, I dropped the act, stared at the $24 bill, crushed it in my hands and threw it.

The search continued. It was wicked dark, and as I embarked on the next portion of my journey, I bumped into a guy who was dancing alone. It turned out to be none other than JD. We gave each other a timid, knowing smile…Seeing him alone made me feel so much better about myself. I think he was relieved, too. "Let's do another shot!" he said, and put his arm around me as we walked to the bar. I'm not sure if we were drinking to have more fun, or to forget about the fun that we weren't having.

We found Khanna, completely shit-faced, dancing a *Bhangra* step to an Enrique Iglesias song in front of two girls, who seemed completely appalled by him. We turned and went the other way, pretending we'd never seen him before. We continued across the dance floor and spotted a guy who was dancing alone like Mithun Chakraborty, spinning his hands and legs in all directions. He stood out in his yellow shirt, red tie, dark blue pants and stark white shoes. Upon closer inspection, we realized we'd found our fourth wing, Satya. He was dancing crazily, as if he were the only man left on earth.

Well, I didn't know about them, but I'd had enough frustration for one night. I was about to give up on the whole venture when I saw a group of three girls dancing on their own. I applied my basic Physics and the volatility is found more in an uneven group. I took it as a sign, and walked up to them with a smile that said, *I am having the time of my life…wanna join me?* It worked! They turned to us and started dancing with more passion than before. I gave myself a little pat on the back. Oh yeah, I got game! One of the girls seemed to show particular interest in me. She was twice my size, but at that point, who cared? My other option was to pretend to sip on an empty Jack and Coke in the corner by myself.

As we danced, she got closer and closer, gradually pushing me until we had reached a pillar. My back slammed against it and she turned her back to me as she steadied herself for some serious moves. I was about to get my very own dose of grinding. I held her waist like I'd done it a thousand times before, and stood there while she bumped and grinded against me. I had never felt this much pleasure in public before. Although there wasn't much of a chance anyone would even notice you in the dark.

We bumped and grinded for the better part of a half an hour and the only words that were going through my head were holy words from the scriptures: "Heaven isn't anywhere but in the present moment." Just as suddenly as she'd taken a liking to me, she was taken away. My thoughts of heaven evaporated as her friend grabbed her away from me and told her they had to leave. She smiled, waved, and left. I didn't even have a chance to ask her for her name and number! I had come to a new world, where people don't mind hooking up without even knowing each other! In my old world, you had to plan your future before you could take any pleasure in the present. Different worlds, indeed!

I, once again, stood in the corner. So casual was that encounter that I wondered if she would have any regrets of not seeing me again. I was back in my senses, having sweated out most of the tequila and a portion of the Jack and Coke. I scanned the room and suddenly all the couples were standing out to me. My heart fluttered as it reminded me…Sonia. My stomach rolled with a sense of knowing. I immediately took out my phone. Twenty-four missed calls! OH NO! I called Sonia back, but it went straight to voicemail. I kept calling and calling, but she didn't answer. I was so worried! She had never called me so many times in a row. Something must have been wrong, but there was nothing I could do.

We decided to call it a night. As it turns out, the biggest challenge after a night at the club is getting a cab. Half the world needed a cab at 2 AM, apparently. After almost an hour of waiting, a cab finally pulled up and waved us in. When I got home, I shuffled to my room with every intention of calling Sonia one more time before falling asleep. But a night of drinking and dancing consumed me, and with my phone nestled solidly in my hand, I crashed. When I woke up the next morning, I was in the same position. I held it up and waited to see if it would ring.

She picked up the phone, FaceTime style, but didn't say a word.

"What happened, honey?" I asked, "I saw all your missed calls and I tried to call you back, but your phone was switched off."

There was a long pause, and she finally said, "I did that on purpose."

"Why? What happened?"

"Where were you last night?" I could see that she was upset.

I didn't want to upset her any more than she already was, so I lied. "Honey, I was sleeping and I had my phone on silent…I woke up in the middle of the night and saw your missed calls. I tried to get a hold of you, but you'd turned your phone off!"

She was silent, and looked as if she didn't believe me. Upon seeing her expression, I decided there was no way I could ever tell her the truth. I was asleep. That was my story and I was sticking to it.

"You know what the date is today?" she asked, as if it was some kind of test.

"Yeah honey," I said, still not getting it. "It's Saturday, the 24th."

She took a long, deep breath and replied ever-so-politely (which shook the hell out of me), "Karti, today is our anniversary. It used to be the biggest day for us. I know you're not here, but I expected you to call, or at the very least answer when I called."

Every nerve ending in my body froze. A wave of emotion came over me – guilt, anxiety, sadness, regret. "Oh my god!" I said, with as apologetic a tone as I could muster. "Happy Anniversary, my cutie! Hey…I love you. Look at me. I'm here now. We'll celebrate today!" She turned away, not allowing me to see her face. Not saying a word. "Hey, please…Soni, I am really, *really* sorry. Shit, how can I..?. I can see that you're hurt, but…"

It was too late. I had broken her trust and I realized my confession couldn't fix it.

"I was so happy all day. I kept telling everyone in the office about our special day, and they were excited for me, too. But when you didn't answer any of my calls, I was heartbroken. I was alone, with no one to share my feelings with. I tried calling you for almost three hours, and then I gave up."

"Oh honey…I am really sorry!"

"Everyone tried to make me feel better, but I couldn't handle their sympathy. At that point, I didn't even want to talk to you anymore, so I switched off my phone. Then when I left word…" She paused a moment, letting the lump of tears pass through her throat. "I saw a person standing at my bike with flowers and a card. It was Raghu. 'What is this?' I asked him. 'Happy Anniversary!' he said. 'I understand that the presence of your beloved is important, and Kartik would have given you these if he was here. Please accept these from me, from your friend on your special day.' After hearing those words I was speechless, and I couldn't stop crying. I wished you had been the one to send those flowers. But you… And I was miserable at the thought that I don't care to be here with the people who care about me. I don't want to be with them, I want to be with you. But you're not here. Where should I go? What the hell should I do?"

It was painful to hear that she felt my absence but it was much more painful that Raghu was placating on my behalf. My intuitions were scaring me down to hell. I was shattered. Both, my friendship and love were on stake. I was able to calm her down by the end of the call. She felt better. All I felt, though, was lost.

LIFE GOES ON...

The semester was ploughing right along, and our routine was set. Group meetings, assignments, seminars, university events and extra-curricular activities were sandwiched by morning jobs and evening classes. We got into the flow, as it were. One day, JD, Satya and I were standing just outside our building discussing our *Basic Economics* class. Don't be fooled by the title. There was nothing basic about it. We were asked to read *The Wall Street Journal* cover-to-cover every day, so we could discuss the articles in class. This was a serious challenge for people who already spoke perfect English, let alone those of us who were ESL students. For our mid-term exam, we were asked to submit an eight-page paper, and we were expressing our angst about the situation when Ron and Sid passed by.

"Hey guys," Ron said, patting me on the shoulder. "Heard you all got jobs. Congrats! How's it going?"

"Good. KJ cleans cars in the parking lot!" JD said.

"Yeah," I said, "and JD washes dishes in food court."

"Haha good... and how are your studies going?"

Satya couldn't contain himself any longer. "Next week is the Economics mid-term paper submission. We need to write eight pages!" he blurted, stress pouring out of his veins.

"Only eight? That's nothing. I used to write fifty pages for a three-hour exam in engineering school. This is child's play."

"Hey *Ratlami* hero," Sid said as he punched my shoulder, "Here, you don't get graded on the amount of pages you write. Here, professors will butcher you if you don't present them with quality writing – writing that takes thought, time and research."

"Yeah Sid, please forgive this under-privileged child!" JD said, poking me.

"Shut up, you…poor waiter," I said, poking him back.

JD, buttering Sid up with a soft, low voice, said, "Sid, buddy, once upon a time we ate chicken off the same plate. Do you mind if I borrow your Basic Eco paper from last year?"

The nerve of some people!

"Sure, if you want to get in trouble," Sid replied.

"Trouble. How come?"

"You can't copy assignments here," Sid answered.

"Then how are we going to complete the assignment?" I asked, simultaneously shocked and disappointed.

Sid just looked at us for a moment, and then he said, "You just have to do it *on your own*. Like an adult."

"But why?" I asked, befuddled by the prospect of having to work hard to get a degree. "The professor won't know about it. And besides, you're giving it to us out of your will, we're not stealing it!"

"The professor will scan your sheet, and if you get caught you could be detained or expelled under the plagiarism rules. You have to do your own research and complete the paper. It has to be concise, informative, and in the proper format without grammatical mistakes."

"Sounds scary!" I said, unable to wrap my head around this concept.

"It'll be good for you. Maybe you'll even learn something!" Sid said, as he patted my back and walked away.

I was so used to seniors helping out, but in this case they scared the crap out of us. This is how the system worked, though, and we had to step up and do our own work.

18

EXAMS AND GRADES! WHAT IS THEIR SIGNIFICANCE?

After a week, the results from the economics exam were in. In my engineering days, the scariest part was not in finding how *I* did in the exam. It was how I did *in comparison* to all of my friends. One always knew, because the scores were published on a board in front of college. This, however, was not the case here.

Professor David Jones entered the classroom with the papers in his hand. He was an elegant gentleman in his late fifties, with a tall, slim build and distinguishing white hair. He always wore a hat, and I wondered if that was to hide the receding hairline, or just a habit he couldn't seem to break. Professor David was an expert in both macro- and micro-economics, and I liked the way he taught, but I didn't know how he graded papers because this was our first one.

He kept the stack of papers folded in his hand, opened the top one to look at the name, and started walking towards me. I closed my eyes, praying it wasn't mine. I heard the sound of his footsteps coming closer, and then there was silence. I opened my eyes to see him standing right next to me, with his hand outstretched.

"Thanks Professor!" I said, as I took the paper from his hand. I was relieved to see that he was distributing the papers individually, and kept them folded so that no one else could see your score. Nobody tried to peer over at your paper to see how you did, nor did they ask you to tell them. Just as those thoughts were going through my mind, I saw JD waving at me from his side of the room. I shrugged and shook my head a little, as if to say, "What do you want?"

He gestured back, my translation of which was, "What was your score?" Like hell, I was going to tell him! Gone were the days of competition and public score results. I was keeping this to myself. I showed him my middle finger, which shut him up.

As I opened the paper, I felt like I had the wind knocked out of me. I could barely see the original blue ink with which I'd written the paper, as it was saturated with red markings from the professor. I flipped to the last page to find the grade: B-minus! My heart sank with disappointment, and I went to the professor after class to find out the reason behind the low grade. He explained it to me so softly and gently, you'd have thought it was he who'd made those errors, not me. Everything he said made sense, and there was nothing left for me but to accept that I'd made mistakes and learn from them. *It is not a failure, but an opportunity to learn…and that's what I am here for.* I carried that thought and by the end I felt okay about my B-minus. The only way to go from here was up.

FESTIVALS AWAY FROM FESTIVITY

A necessary addition to any degree program, especially one in a foreign country, is the extra-curricular activities. Taking part in a variety of clubs and organizations leads to friendships, community, and even the feeling of having an extended family of sorts. The university provided the funds, and the students ran the clubs. We had the Graduate Professional Network (GPN), Entrepreneurship Development Center (EDC), Afro-Americans Society (AAS), Islamic Youth, Graduate Students Association (GSA), Community for International Students (CIS), and of course, the Graduate Indian Students Association (GISA). There were almost 70 organizations to choose from, each one with its own purpose, and a dedicated yearly budget to achieve their goals. Any student could join any organization based on interest, which allowed for a whole other level of education that wasn't restricted to a defined set of books, but rather an infinite pool of knowledge and exposure. These clubs also provided an opportunity to build your professional network, which we all know is an absolute necessity for any entrepreneur. As they always say, "Greater success comes with a healthier network."

I began to understand why, with only three three-hour classes per week, they dared call it a full-time MBA. At first, I thought it should have been called a *quarter-time* MBA. But when I saw the number of events happening throughout the year, and the various organizations I could be a part of, I realized that education extended far beyond the classroom. Even with the light class load, I did not find myself with much free time once I got involved with the extra-curricular stuff.

It was November, the month of *Diwali* in India, where the atmosphere was surely filled with festivity and celebration. But in the US, we were busy attending lectures and doing assignments; nothing festive about that. GISA did organize a *Diwali* celebration on campus, but that lasted only a day, rather than a month. We did a *Diwali* prayer at the beginning of the celebration. There was dancing, music and an array of celebratory food. All Indians in attendance donned traditional attire to make the celebration seem authentic. A few foreign friends joined us and it was fun to show others a side of our culture they didn't know about. People were having fun, and seemed to be happy. But there was definitely something missing. I guess festivals are incomplete without having family around to celebrate with you. But, to make the best out of it, there were several performances, which expressed different sides of Indian culture. I was surprised to find that I was filled with pride, watching these performances and seeing the non-Indian among us being simultaneously entertained and educated.

After the performances were over, I finally made it over to the buffet that served Indian food. I helped myself to *Naan, Kadhai Paneer, Malai Kofta, Daal Makhani, Jeera Rice, Idli-Sambhar, Gulab Jamun* and *Paan.* It was the first time in months I'd seen all these dishes together on one table. I felt, for just a moment, that I was back in India and it gave me a warm feeling in my stomach. That also might have been all the food I'd just wolfed down, but that's a lot less romantic.

EXAM OR A TREAT?

The first semester was coming to an end, and all that was left were the final exams. I remember the most common offense amongst students in engineering school was to take a cheat sheet into the exam hall. If you got caught, you would receive detention, the length of which would depend on the length of the cheat sheet. Kabeer used to prepare for the exams by shoving cheat sheets in every crevice from his socks to his underwear to his collarbone. During the exam itself, he'd spend half the time in search of the right one.

But in the US, things were different. During the last economics class before the final exam, Professor David actually instructed us to bring a cheat sheet! As long as it was no larger than 8.5 by 11, it was completely legal. *You kidding me!* It was an exam treat. I guess the trick was getting the right information on that sheet of paper.

On the day of the exam, JD, Satya and I decided to sit next to each other so that we could secretly help each other write the paper. Unfortunately, we were late, and instead, found seats in the three extreme corners of the room. My confidence seeped right out of me the way a balloon loses its air when one loosens the knot. Even though I had prepared a cheat sheet with the smallest possible font, I still found myself filled to the brim with fear. I always trusted my friends more than my own preparation. I sat frozen as Professor David distributed the exam sheets.

He hadn't gotten to me yet when I felt someone's eyes on me, so I turned to find Fu Li sitting next to me. She gave a smile and quickly averted her eyes, afraid, I'm sure, of being accused of cheating. Though short-lived, her sweet smile made me forget my nervousness. I turned to my desk with a newfound confidence, and was surprised to find that the exam was relatively easy. More than half of the questions were multiple choice, which, with the cheat sheet in hand, were easy for me to answer. After only five minutes, the professor disappeared from the classroom. *You kidding me, again?* I thought. *What kind of exam is this?* I had never before taken an exam in which a cheat sheet was perfectly acceptable, and the teacher left the room! An exam without a monitor? Unheard of! I soon realized that everyone was focused on their own work, as if they didn't really know what cheating was. After feeling extremely uptight and anxious for the first fifteen minutes of the exam, I took a deep breath and thought to myself, *"Dude! The exam is easy. There is no one to compete against but yourself, and on top of it all, the professor isn't even in the room!"* That thought allowed me to relax into the exam. It seemed that my mind was working more efficiently than ever.

But that wasn't all. The very next day, we had to take the Marketing exam. Professor Steven was distributing the exam when Katie, my pretty classmate, asked him with her charming, irresistible smile, if we could do a take-home exam. Blake and a few other students spoke up in agreement, but I stayed silent because I didn't know what the hell they were talking about. Professor Steven thought for a moment, and finally said, "Okay, you may take the exam home and submit it tomorrow in my office by 5 PM."

Wait. What just happened? I confirmed with Blake, "Does he mean we can take this and do it at home?"

"Yeah bro!" he said, with a big smile on his face. "This is now a take-home exam. Just turn it in tomorrow at his office."

I bet you think I'm kidding now! I felt like a thief who'd been given the keys to a mansion.

Even with these seemingly lackadaisical rules, I found that I retained far more than I had, back at engineering school. After one of those exams, nearly everything went out of our heads. But in this case, I wasn't just regurgitating information to get a passing grade, I was learning the new system that would help me succeed – both in business and in life.

AT THE IDENTITY OF AMERICA

It was December, and the long semester break was upon us. Five months had gone by; five long months away from home, without seeing my family. They wanted me to visit, naturally, and Sonia was desperately expecting me to come and wrap her in my arms. Unfortunately, it was also the peak time for tourism in India and plane tickets were astronomically high. With a hefty loan hanging over my head, not to mention a few unexpected, and unbudgeted, Apple purchases, the cost of the trip would have been looming eerily in the back of my mind. I wouldn't have been able to enjoy the time I'd spend in India had I gone back with this, even if it *would* include being with family and Sonia. It was simultaneously a tremendously difficult decision, and a no-brainer. I would have to stay in Boston.

Natasha and Khanna went to India for the month, while Shalini, JD, Satya and I formed a motley band of adventurous folks.

On the morning of December 31, we boarded a bus to New York City. On the way to The Big Apple, it was refreshing to see the sights and sounds of nature. Living in a city like Boston, you almost forget that such vegetation exists. The bus dropped us off in China Town, and it was bustling and bursting with people. We almost felt as if we were back home in India! The movies I'd seen depicting New York made it look much less crowded and noisy than it actually was. We got off the bus and found the nearest subway, excited to go to the destination for which NYC is most famous – Times Square. The train was just as crowded as any Mumbai local, the only the difference being that they were comfortably air-conditioned. There were no people hanging off the sides of the train and the doors were able to close.

We got off at 42nd Street, and as we emerged from the subway, we were slapped with sub-zero temperatures and the most vibrant energy I'd ever experienced. You could *feel* the magic in the air. People were ecstatic about New Year's Eve. All the roads in and around Times Square were blocked and people were flooding to the site of the famous Ball, which would drop a total of 141 feet from the building at #1, Times Square, at midnight. It was now 5 PM, and there were already so many people congregating for the festivities. It was nearly impossible to navigate the streets. The sun had already gone down and people were bundled up to the point that only their eyes peeked out of their winter gear. But it didn't matter. It was all part of the fun.

Times Square is known for being the headquarters for some of the top-notch global companies such as Coke, Kodak, Thompson Reuters, Yahoo, Chase, Chevrolet, etc. Standing in the middle of Times Square, looking around, I felt like I'd just entered some kind of Commercial Wonderland. The sun may have set, but Times Square shone brighter than daylight with walls of lighted signs and advertisements that were in constant motion. Even in our sardine-like state, people could not pass up the chance to take pictures at every angle. Satya and I designated the job of photographer extraordinaire to JD and Shalini. As they raised their cameras, Satya posed as if he'd been recruited to work for whatever company's name was visible behind him. Seeing this utterly brilliant scam, I joined him. This was a big moment for two from the tiny towns of India. The four of us were wandering like children set free in Disneyland. Of course, not to forget the virtual world, we immediately posted our photos on Facebook with the caption, "Craziest New Year ever!"

By 11:45 PM, we were stuck in a sardine sandwich. It was probably for the best, since it was freezing outside. The proximity of the others around made the bone chilling weather just slightly more bearable. But there was nowhere to go without disrupting the crowd around you. If one person moved, the entire crowd shifted to accommodate the change. The ball was about to drop. The excitement in the air was palpable. Finally, the clock needles edged to 11:59 PM and the ball began to drop. People screamed with shock and awe, and I heard someone in the crowd say that it felt like a meteor had passed by the earth without touching the ground. The countdown from 11:59 and 50 seconds to midnight turned out to be ten of the most exciting, anticipatory seconds I'd ever experienced. The crowd screamed so loudly together that it almost sounded the same as silence – "10! 9! 8! 7! 6! 5! 4! 3! 2! 1! Happy New Year!" The atmosphere was filled with celebration.

That Facebook caption wasn't a hyperbole. It was, in fact, the biggest New Year's celebration I had ever been a part of. We hung out all night on the streets of Manhattan.

JD, as usual, was stuck like glue to Shalini the whole time. I could sense the butterflies in his stomach.

While I was stalking JD's love, Satya was busy taking photographs. All of a sudden, the darkness turned to a slow burst of light – the sun was rising. We'd been having so much fun that we didn't even notice it was already morning.

Now that it was already daylight, we decided that we might as well visit the face of US – the Statue of Liberty. We took the ferry, of course, and as we got closer and closer, pride started to well up in all of us. This is where we live! After the beautiful green giant with the torch, we walked across the Brooklyn Bridge, where *Kal Ho Na Ho* and many other movies we loved were shot. Then it was time to visit the world-famous Madame Tussaud's Wax Museum, an opportunity to see the world's most popular celebrities up close: Mahatma Gandhi, Michael Jackson, Arnold Schwarzenegger, Tom Cruise, Marylin Monroe, Shahrukh Khan and the list goes on. And of course we took lots of photos with them. Satya held all the female stars in his arms for the pictures whereas JD only had eyes for Shalini to make her realize she is more important than all other stars around. And last but not least – the street food of New York.

And thus our trip ended, with the memories of the Best New Year's Ever.

19

SECOND SEMESTER: THE WATER IS GETTING DEEPER!

It was January and the second semester had begun. Every day of the past five months had been a new experience. In the sixth month, I found that student life had settled down and there were no longer surprises lurking around every corner, or lessons to be learned at each turn. Of course, the new semester brought new courses, professors, peers and colleagues, but the routine remained the same.

The roommate bond was as strong as ever. Our two favorite places to chill out at were our own apartment, and the Bayside. One thing that made our bond strong was *hookah.* If someone told us that the world was ending the next day, our last wish would be to enjoy one more hookah puff together. It was also Natasha's favorite post-dinner activity, and gave us an excuse to invite them over, almost excessively. We grew even closer as friends, and the bond we built was as good as having family away from family. My parking job stayed constant, and my English became more and more fluent, as I spent time listening to Jimmy and Terrell's early morning gossip.

On the other side of the world, Sonia was getting busier by the day with her new job. Our conversations were limited to "Good morning," "Good evening," "How was your day?" And sometimes, if her energy level allowed, she would share her office stories and familial concerns.

Calling home also became part of my routine as I settled in more and more into life in the US. I would call my mother more often than I called my father, because she would actually talk to me. My father had only the usual questions and lectures to share; the question bank for me was from his favorite sections on work and studies. I also spoke to Aditi from time to time. She loved talking about her school life and enjoyed bitching about the fun I had without her.

THE FIRST PROFESSIONAL EXPERIENCE

Though it was still winter, it was time to begin the search for paid summer internships. Internships are the first rung on any corporate ladder, and are an important part of an MBA student's life for many reasons: they give you an opportunity to gain work experience build your résumé, pay the bills during summer when your other job isn't there to give you hands-on career and networking experience, and greatly increase your chances of getting a full-time job sooner rather than later. One evening, I had gone down the summer intern rabbit hole on the Internet, and was completely lost. It felt more like a black hole. I decided to turn to Ron for assistance.

"Hey! Come in my *Ratlami* bro! How are you?" Ron said, seeing me at his door, forlorn and pathetic.

"Okay," I said. "I'm searching for summer internships right now." We sat on the couch.

"Oh wonderful, in which field?" asked Ron.

"Marketing," I said confidently.

"Why marketing?" he asked, with a daunting and concerned look on his face.

"I worked my ass off to escape the IT graveyard back home! I'm more interested in going out and meeting new people, while doing my job," I answered, feeling confident in my well thought-out answer.

"So…why did you come to the US?"

"What do you mean?" I could feel my confidence starting to fall.

Ron put his hand on my shoulder and said with kindness, "Look, you have to understand the basics of a job search in the US, especially for international students. It has nothing to do with what you want to do, but rather what the US wants you to do for them."

"So what does the US want me to do for them?" I asked.

"IT!" he said. Fuck.

"But…It's an internship. Shouldn't I be doing something I'm interested in but don't necessarily possess the honed skills to do? Isn't that the point of an internship? To build those new skills? And besides, marketing is the core of any industry, not IT!"

"That's all very well, but in the global market they are the leaders in designing, managing and selling their products. When it comes to communication, it's important to be completely, 100% fluent and not just proficient in English. English as a first language is almost a prerequisite for marketing jobs. Anyway, apart from good English, the basis of marketing is *building relationships* and how you build relationships?"

"Umm…"

"By connecting the dots! How would you connect the dots?" I didn't know. He continued after I gave him a blank stare. "Using points from history, politics, pop culture, sports and inside jokes, because that's the kind of stuff that strikes an emotional chord. How would someone from a foreign country be able to relate on an interpersonal level using these tactics?" I shrugged. "Okay, tell me, do Americans know who Shahrukh Khan is?"

"Most of them do, I should hope," I said.

"Okay. How about Mithun or Altaf Raja?"

"Haha, no way," I laughed.

"Do they know ads like *Dhara dhara shuddh dhara?* TV shows like *Kapil Sharma Comedy Nights,* or *Chandrakanta?* Movies like *Sholay, DDLJ, or Black?* Political parties such as *BJP, AAP* and *Congress?* What about cricket? Would you be able to talk to any American at length about cricket? Do they know about the best innings played by Sachin Tendulkar?"

He had me at *Chandrakanta,* but I let him rattle on. I was very entertained by his in-depth explanation, and it actually started making a lot of sense, as much as it pained me to admit it.

"Now, if you asked any American to go to India and build a network, what would you expect to happen?

Disaster, right? It's not enough to know about product, there needs to be a complete understanding of the market and an almost empathetic connection with the buyer. If you can't connect the dots, it becomes challenging to understand the market in-depth and build a strategy. It's not impossible, but it is important to keep in mind before diving into the job ocean."

"Makes sense. So how does IT work for us, then?" My voice became more humble.

"Because Indians make up a large portion of the IT world, and we come pretty cheap. India keeps spitting out IT experts while the US encourages people to choose the profession they're actually interested in. I guess most Americans aren't interested in standing under the IT umbrella. What better option than to entertain budget-friendly, utterly sufficient IT applicants from India?"

"Awesome, I never thought of it that way. So what should I do now?" I asked, wanting to go home with a clear purpose.

"You already have preliminary experience. That's great. Create a résumé showing your experience in reporting, data warehousing, JAVA,.NET, and whatever else you think might make you stand out from the other applicants."

"Okay. Then what?"

"Learn them…Haha…I call this reverse engineering!"

"Oh no, not again!" I didn't want to go back in the same graveyard.

"Why? You don't like IT?"

"Let's put it this way: if you gave me two options – go to bed hungry or have a delicious Indian meal after doing some IT work, I would go for the first option."

Ron didn't seem to understand that this was a little version of my own private hell. I was being pulled towards the same circle that I worked so hard to escape. But since I took a big financial risk coming to the US, I had no option but to choose something that would generate the highest paycheck. And hey, if I could work in parking, I could work in IT, I guess.

The discussion changed my entire perspective. I went home and continued my search, only this time I had much different criteria.

THE CRAZIEST NIGHT

The most common topic, when trying to break the ice, is weather! That started making more sense to me as the winter hit the lowest temperatures I'd ever experienced. Suddenly, I wanted to talk about the weather, too. To get ready for work in the morning, I had to put on long underwear, long pants and a long-sleeved shirt, a woolen sweater, snow boots, gloves, a thin cozy, inner jacket, topped with a thick jacket with had a hood that I pulled over a second woolen hat. Any skin left uncovered was bound to freeze, as temperatures fell below 0 degree Celsius. Add the wind chill factor and you might as well be in Antarctica. Seriously!

But this morning was different. I put on all my gear as usual, and as I stepped out of the building, I saw nothing but white ahead of me. All the trees and cars were covered. It was as if someone had drawn a powdery white curtain over my eyes. A new phrase was added to my vocabulary that day: "It's snowing!" I couldn't help but say it out loud, even though there was no one around to hear me. I reached the parking lot. Jimmy and Terrell were already there, chatting about this and that as the cars came in.

"Hey man, what are you up to this weekend?" Jimmy asked, while collecting cash from a driver that had just pulled up to the booth.

"Nothing much. How about you?"

"Don't you know? We're having a party. It's Terrell's Birthday, dude."

"Your birthday? You didn't even tell me, *ass*," I said as I punched Terrell playfully in the shoulder.

"I was about to, bro. This fool beat me to the punch."

"Okay, whatever. So what's the plan?" I wouldn't pass up a chance to celebrate.

"HOUSE PARTY!" said Terrell. "Tomorrow at nine."

Who knew? The craziest fun in the US is not found in clubs, pubs, or bars, but at undergrad house parties with youngsters full of passion and enthusiasm! Since most attendees were under 21, it became a law-free zone where under-aged folks can get sloshed, puke, scream and go generally crazy.

I wore a black T-shirt and jeans, and put on all types of colognes that were in my closet. I heard that birthdays in the US are celebrated differently than in India, but this was going to be my first real experience. In the US, I heard, the birthday boy's friends are supposed to treat him. They buy drinks if they're having a house party, and if they go out to a restaurant, each pays for himself PLUS a portion of the birthday boy's meal. When I first heard this, I was surprised. What's the point of going to a party if it's not *free*? But the Americans I spoke with about this, thought *we* were equally crazy for having a tradition where the birthday boy treats all of his friends. "What's the point of celebrating a birthday if you have to pay for everything?" they asked. I guess the way you grew up was the way that seemed most normal. Even though I thought it was weird, I got a six-pack of beer and headed to the party.

From downstairs, I could hear loud music and excited banter coming from the apartment. I followed the sound and eventually reached Terrell's place. My excitement was triggered as I rang the doorbell. A young girl in a tight miniskirt opened the door, hung on to me, and gave me an extremely tight hug. Clearly, she was drunk. I gently set her aside after an awkwardly long hug, and entered. The apartment was dimly lit and was filled with people, noise, flashing lights and loud woofers pumping sounds that would be undecipherable to people who were no longer in college. It reminded me of a smaller version of the *Club Jaz.*

Jimmy popped up in front of me: "Hey dude, come on in!" Standing next to him was a guy with cake all over his face. Upon closer inspection, I realized it was Terrell. The party had certainly begun for him.

"Come on, let's go get some drinks!" They led me to the kitchen where a variety of beverages were scattered about on the counter. I joined a group doing shots, and we each had four shots back-to-back. As the alcohol took hold of my senses, all I wanted to do was dance, jump and scream and do all the other crazy stuff that everyone else was doing. I guess I had caught their frequency! I grabbed a cold beer and went into the hallway, where a small crowd was smoking a hookah. As small as the crowd was, the hallway was even smaller, so I continued to the corner bedroom, curious to see what was going on in there.

As I entered, I saw two girls rolling around on top of one guy on the bed. In the corner, there was a couple smooching, and next to them, another small group was dancing. Not one of them seemed to notice, or care, that there were other people doing other things in the same room. This was even more awkward than the lengthy hug I received upon my arrival, so I moved on. I came upon two bathrooms, both of which had open doors, but were most certainly occupied. Hugging the porcelain god doesn't even begin to cover it. In another room, two guys were playing a game called *beer pong*. It took a moment of observation to see how this game worked, but it seemed quite fun. Cups filled with beer were placed on both ends of a table, and you had to bounce a ping pong ball and make it into the cup. If you won, you had to drink. If you lost, you had to drink twice. Now that was a drinking game!

In another corner of the room, there stood a keg of beer. I watched as four people dragged Terrell to the keg, held him upside down, plugged the open tap in his mouth and started counting down from twenty. Poor Terrell struggled to gulp down the beer, but when they reached four, he finally gave up. I don't think I would have even lasted that long! He was a champ for enduring such abuse on his birthday.

As I was looking around the room for a group to join and chat with, Jimmy patted me from behind, "Hey man, what's up?" Before I could even respond, four guys held me from my limbs and tipped me upside down. It was my turn. They held me so tight, I could hardly move. The pressure of the tap was so intense I felt as if they were pouring beer directly into my brain. I gave up at five. Unable to feel my own body or recognize any faces in the crowd, I silently sat on the couch. I'm not sure how long I sat there, but when I came back to my senses I found two girls in black dresses and high heels sitting next to me. We exchanged glances and smiles.

"Are you alright?" asked the first.

"Yeah, not bad. Not bad," If this was the after-effect, I could do this keg-stand thing more often. "I am Kartik, by the way, you can call me KJ." I said, glad that my brain was working well enough to remember my own name.

"I'm Jessica."

"And I'm Laura."

"You go to UMass?" this was my patent question to kick start the conversation.

"Yeah. I'm Jimmy's friend. We took an Art and Design course together," said Jessica.

"I'm Terrell's girlfriend!" Laura chimed in. "I go to Boston University." Oh yeah! I then remembered her face from a whole slew of photos he'd shown me one day at work. She was, in fact, one of his girlfriends, but she said it so proudly that I didn't want to burst her bubble.

"How about you?" asked Jessica

"I'm at UMass, getting my MBA."

"Oh my god, that's amazing!" She began to pamper me. In the US, getting a Master's degree is a big deal, because most students go deep into debt doing so, unlike in India, where parents bear the brunt of the cost of such things.

I grabbed a hookah off the table and inhaled a long, thick puff. Jessica was impressed. "Oh you're a master! I never saw this much smoke before!" She was drunk, but I was happy that she was impressed by me all the same. Jimmy and Laura were smoking something out of a smaller pipe. After every puff, they'd cough and laugh. I just stared at them, trying to figure out what was happening. Jimmy offered me the pipe.

"What's that?" I asked, innocently.

"Man, this is life!" Jimmy answered, looking at me with bright red eyes.

"No man, I'm good," I had never smoked anything stronger than flavored tobacco from a hookah.

Jimmy said, "Brother, remember! This night is about acceptance, not abstinence; fun, not fundamentals; and experience, not escape…and yes, this moment will never come again!" It was a convincing argument. I reached for the pipe, inhaled a long puff (as I would do from a hookah) and started coughing uncontrollably.

"There you go, bro!" said Jimmy, laughing at my expense.

Within a few moments, the world became perceptively slower. I could hear every word as if it were said slowly and clearly just for my ears. Every sound was so refined.

It felt as if David Guetta was playing especially for me. I was unable to move; my body was completely stoned. I was doomed.

Jessica started talking about spirituality and metaphysics, which I was far from being able to comprehend in that moment. I was pretty sure even she didn't know what she was saying. Even so, I couldn't help but smile, sit back and enjoy this one-sided conversation. After a while, she said she felt suffocated and asked me to go downstairs with her for some fresh air. It was chilly outside. I felt like we were locked in a freezer. She lit a cigarette, took a nice, long drag and offered it to me. Might as well do it! I'd already inhaled more than my fair share of foreign substances, why stop now? I took a conservative puff, not wanting to have a repeat performance of the uncontrollable coughing, but to no avail. I could not hold back the choking cough that began before the cigarette was even out of range of my lips. It was embarrassing, but she didn't seem to mind. With a cute smile she came close to me, held the cigarette up to my lips and said, "Now take it easy, honey." She was so close to me that I could barely think. I was completely lost in her eyes. After an eternity, she said, "Ahem. Ahem… hello? The cigarette is finished!" She took it from my lips and smashed it to the ground.

This was my otherworldly experience with a stunning beauty in the dark, chilled moonlight. In the influence of the moment, I gently pushed her towards the wall and looked into her eyes. My heart felt like it was beating faster than ever before.

With a romantic gaze, I said: "Jess, I think I love you."

She exploded with laughter. "Haha! Are you kidding me? You don't even know me, how could you love me?" It was strange to see her taking my words so insincerely. She playfully grabbed my arm and led me to the stairs located at the back of the building. It was 3:30 AM and all else was silent in the dark night. While climbing to the fifth floor, our breath grew faster and warmer. I don't know if it was the booze or the smoke, or having been upside down with beer pumping into my veins, but I had to sit down. I wasn't going to make it up those stairs in one haul. I needed to rest. She sat with me, looked me right in the eyes, came close to me and clinched my shirt in her hand, pulling me even closer. Gradually, I found my cold, dry lips had melted into her glossy ones. I pushed her to the wall and grabbed her waist tight. The chilled weather brought us even closer. There was no space between us. There was nothing around us. We were lost in each other. My hands crawled upwards towards her…and suddenly we heard the sound of clomping footsteps approach. We instantly separated and looked around. Those clomping footsteps belonged to a cop, which scared the hell out of me.

"Do you live here?" he asked, trying to keep his booming voice down out of respect for the sleeping neighbors.

I swallowed hard and replied, "Um…Yeah."

"All right, sorry to bother you," and he was gone.

I was surprised and thought, *"Wait! You're not gonna harass, bribe or frighten me?"* If all cops were like this, then surely they are good for the society, despite their less-than-favorable reputation. Good Old America!

It was getting late and Jessica had to leave. I walked her to her car and felt that she was completely into me.

"I really like you!" she said, totally validating what I already felt to be true.

"I like you, too," I said, giddy with excitement.

"And, yeah…" she began, but then just sat there, looking at me.

"What?" I asked.

"You are a sexy kisser…I think I wanna have sex with you!" GULP!

Controlling my anxiety I gave her a smile and said, "See you soon."

And she was off. In her little blue car that seemed perfectly suited for her.

With Jessica out of sight, I let the anxiety overtake me. My whole body was shaking! In India, it used to take years to reach to this stage. First year, follow her on your bike. Second year, propose to her, saying "I love you" and bringing her flowers and gifts. Third year, have some luck giving and receiving kisses. Fourth year, you either get married, or you break up. But it was quite the opposite here. Here, couples start with the physical, then continue until they either fall in love or break up. And break ups are as normal as changing clothes. I grew up watching Bollywood movies, so I believed in love at first sight, but I would have to get used to this new practice of sex at first sight.

As soon as I reached home, I felt a pang of guilt as Sonia's sweet, soft voice wafted into my mind. I breathlessly checked my phone. No call! I was surprised. She seemed to always know when I was making a connection on this side of the world, and she'd make sure to call me and insist that

I talk to her. Tonight was different. No phone call. It should have been a good thing, but I found myself with a wee bit of discomfort in my stomach. I decided to call her to see what was going on in her world.

"Hey Soni."

"Hey Karti."

"I was waiting for your call," I said in a subtly desperate tone.

"Hey baby sorry, I am with Raghu. It's his dad's birthday today, so I was just helping him with preparations for the party."

"Oh, Raghu, huh?"

"C'mon, it's not like that," she said.

"Okay, seems you don't have time, then" I said in an angrier tone than I had intended.

"Kartik, what happened? I really didn't have the chance to call you. It happens."

"It's fine. Carry on with your celebration!" My voice got feeble.

"Karti, look – *Hey Raghu, yeah that cake is better* – Yeah Kartik, sorry, we are at the cake shop in the middle of selecting a cake, so…"

"Oh. Okay, so when will you…"

"Hey Kartik, I'm sorry. I have to go. I'll call you some other time. Bye."

She hung up. Without even waiting for my *goodbye, take care.* Something was different. She never would have done that before. I felt awful. I remembered how, before, she would sometimes even skip dinner just to talk to me. And now she was skipping my call to pick out a cake for someone else? The pit in my stomach grew larger and larger, and I tried to calm myself with the thought that in my absence she needed to make friends and stay occupied. I shouldn't take it personally. This is what I wanted! For her to live her life and not be so attached to mine! But now that it was happening, I found myself angry at the prospect that she didn't need me anymore; that she was letting me go. The only person flashed back to my mind was Jess. The karma was acting right then and there. There was nothing left for me to defend. The circumstances were taking me to the destination that I never imagined and would never prefer to happen.

20

WHAT MAKES THE USA A SUPERPOWER?

Since the day I landed in the US, the most common discussion was the comparison between India and the US. In everyday banter Indians often compared the two countries in terms of culture, education, politics, food, attitude and development. It is natural to compare because that is what one tends to do. While the population of the US is about 25% of that of India, the United States is ahead in terms of development and technology by at least twenty-five years. The differences are bound to attract some attention.

One day, I went to the food court at lunchtime. Coincidentally, Ron was there too, and I invited him to join me. We grabbed the corner table where, through the glass wall, we could see the spectacular bay gleaming in the sun. He asked me about classes and my parking job. I asked him what he thought attracted people to the US.

"Blonds," he winked as he took a sip of his Coke.

"Haha, you're right about that. But seriously, about 150 years ago all the countries were pretty much on the same page in terms of growth and development. Today, though, the US has become the superpower. What do you think is the core reason behind it?"

He brought the glass close to his mouth, stopped before taking a sip, and looked at me, "You really wanna know?"

"Yeah, of course." From past experience, I expected Ron to say something mind-blowing.

"Well Kartik, there are several reasons. But if you want to know about just one, then…"

"IT!" I said confidently.

"No."

"Infrastructure?"

"No." He raised his index finger and said, "That one reason…"

"What is it?" I asked impatiently, giving up the guessing game

He paused, scrunched his thoughtful eyes and said, "Research!"

"Research? How do you mean?" I straightened up my back, ready to listen.

"Research in any field – be it science, technology, IT, medicine, genetics, psychology, archeology, social science, or any number of other fields that we can't even imagine. The US is based on the concept of research, as compared with India, which is based on the concept of following.

"How so?" I asked. I looked down at my pizza, wanting to take a bite, but not wanting anything to distract myself from hearing Ron's explanation, either.

Ron continued, "In any product market, there are basically two kinds of participants: designers and manufacturers. A design may be completely unique, whereas manufacturing is assembly-line, and oriented towards mass-production. Today, the US is the designer, and rest of the world, especially Asia, is the manufacturers of those designs. Those designs are the outcome of research."

"Makes sense, but aren't both equally important to the final outcome?"

"Well, sure. But *importance* and *profit-sharing* are two very different things. Wherever there is research, there is a brain (or brains) involved. Wherever there is a brain involved; there is a price increase. Let's take a layman analogy. In any organization, the richest employees of a company are the core scientists and strategy makers, then the managers, then the supervisors and then, finally, the laborers. The more they use their brain, the higher the salary. It's similar to a computer. The processor is the most expensive element of any computer. The rest of its parts can be manufactured anywhere in the world, but the processor was invented, modified and fabricated in the US. This invention is the outcome of research."

"But how did it all start? We could have also been amazing researchers ourselves, right?"

"Whether you're a designer or a manufacture is a direct correlation of how you were taught. Were you taught to follow or design? If you grew up in India, you were taught to follow. As simple as that."

"It all started with that teacher-student tradition called *Guru-Shishya Parampara*," Ron continued, "where the teacher teaches and the student follows blindly. These days, the concept of following has trickled down among peers as well. Indians know best how to *get* the analytical answers, but they are not taught *what to do* with them. Getting a Master's degree has become a default; a societal requirement. Sharma*ji* proudly announces, "My son has completed his Master's!" and then Gupta*ji* goes home and demands that his son complete his Master's from an even better college than Sharma*ji's* son. This fever has become viral in India. When it comes to research, the only path is a PhD. which is nothing but a decent gateway to becoming a high-salaried professor. And that's how the *concept of following* was built and continues to permeate in society. The most essential factor missing from education in India is the encouragement of a unique way of thinking. That's what we call research."

"Awesome, I'd never thought about it like this! You should really write a book."

"Oh, yeah, right. Very funny."

I wanted to encourage him, because I really did like what he had to say on the matter. I thought other people would, too! "No, I am serious!" I said, finally taking a bite of my now cold pizza.

"Okay, maybe I will. Just let me finish my burger first." He smiled.

KEEP YOUR FREE TREAT! I WANT SOMETHING MORE...

Research is not mere philosophy. The US government spends billions of dollars a year on it, through grants, funding support and subsidization. Thus, I came upon the job title of Research Assistant, or RA. RAs are graduate students, like me, who spend every waking hour hunting for a job. This hunt is by far the most intense, but also the most lucrative if you are successful. First, the paycheck hikes from about $10 an hour at the parking garage to nearly $20 an hour. Second, you become eligible to have your tuition fees waived, anywhere from a quarter to a full ride. Plus, you get to do something awesome – assist world-renowned researchers and become a part of a greater think tank. More incentive, more money. And to have even a small part of my tuition fee waived would take a huge load off my mind.

So, I began to hunt, silently, so as not to alert my ever-nosy roommates and create more competition for myself.

One evening, Khanna, JD and I were cooking dinner after a long day of work, classes and extra-curricular activities. Satya came home and said, "Guys, we're not cooking tonight."

"We aren't cooking for you anyway!" Khanna laughed as he continued to check on his rice.

"Gentlemen, we are going out for dinner tonight."

"Sure, if it's on you," JD said, putting down the wooden spoon he held like a weapon.

"It is," Satya said, "let's go."

We stared at him with surprise. How could this otherwise stingy guy agree to lose his pocket on us? We went back to cooking, thinking that all this was a mean joke. Satya took a bite of raw carrot and said, "Guys, I got a new job!" We all looked at him. He smiled and showed us bits of carrot in his teeth. "RA," he said with a proud roll of his shoulders.

"WHATT?"

"Are you FUCKING KIDDING me?" JD picked up the wooden spoon again.

"You dark horse!" I said, not wanting to be quite as jealous as I was.

"No way *Gulti*," Khanna chimed in, not wanting to be left out of the equation.

I felt as if someone had given me an electric shock. The three of us were simply stunned. JD stopped making chapatti, I dropped the onion I was busily chopping up, and Khanna froze, hovering over the rice cooker.

"What? Where? How?" We were still frozen with surprise.

Satya said, "I just found out today. I'll be working for the Department of Nursing and Health Science."

"Are you gonna work as a nurse or what?" What was an IT engineer going to do in the Nursing department?

"Haha no, I will be working as a data analyst under Professor Sharon Gilbert who is doing research on Healthcare and Quality. Her department has collected data from all the medical schools in Massachusetts. She needs my assistance in data processing and analysis," said Satya.

"Sounds interesting. How did you get this position?" JD asked. My ears perked up.

"My lab supervisor referred me."

"How much will they pay you?" I asked.

"Twenty bucks an hour," beamed Satya.

"Oh my god, wow! And what about tuition?" asked JD.

"My 100% fee is waived," Satya said with a shrug, as though that were the least of it.

We were dumbfounded. None of us could speak.

"Now stop cooking and go get ready. We're celebrating tonight," said Satya. "On me!"

But I wasn't thinking about a free dinner. I was thinking about how in the hell I was going to get an RA position. I don't think my supervisor at the parking lot would even think of referring me for a position like that, nor would he have any reason to. My mind was flooded with possible strategies. While the four of us were out to dinner, celebrating, I had a hard time accepting this free treat when all I wanted was his job.

21

BEACH, BEAUTY AND BOSTON

The very next day, I started searching for RA positions. As I typed 'Departments in UMass Boston,' a message popped up on my mobile screen – *"Want to hang out this weekend? – Jess"*

Oh, Jess! I was glad to hear from her.

"Yeah, sure; -)" I replied.

"Cool. See you on Saturday at 3 PM; -)"

I continued to search for jobs, but I found myself distracted by the thought of Jess. Saturday couldn't come soon enough.

Finally, Saturday it was! It was a beautifully sunny afternoon and I wore a flowery short-sleeved shirt and a pair of light-colored shorts. I was ready and waiting at 2:45 PM. On time for the very first time. Early, in fact!

"I'm here, but I don't see you!" she texted at 3 on the dot.

For some reason, I expected her to come to my door (not meet me downstairs), so I rushed to get a jacket (it would be cold by evening) and bounded down the stairs. There she was, perfectly suited to her spectacularly blue Mini-Cooper convertible. She stepped out and gave me a warm hug, "Good to see you."

Winter was shedding its effect which allowed for skimpier clothing. She wore a sleeveless black top and light pink short-skirt. Her legs were shining like pearls.

"Where are we going?" I rolled my seat back so my legs would fit.

"I'm not telling you," she smirked.

"Ah, so you're kidnapping me?"

She winked at me and stepped on the gas. She drove towards the secluded mountains where only echoes live. We drove uphill, and then back down the other side where there appeared a long, lean beach and an endless, mesmerizing ocean. I could see only the bluest sky and the clearest ocean water in front of me, tall mountains behind me, and beautiful Jess right next to me.

She parked the car near the beach and as we walked along the sand, we found a small cave-like alcove where we set up the camping tent that she'd brought. We'd stopped along the way to get a bottle of wine and a pizza, but I was completely oblivious to the plan at that point. I liked this surprise. It was romantic. She opened her laptop and put on some romantic instrumental music with a soothing mix of saxophone, acoustic piano and violin. It struck at all my romantic chords. We sat close together on the sand, letting the music and let the beauty of the scenery wash over us. I took a deep breath in, smelling the crisp clean ocean air.

"What made you do all this?" I asked.

"Don't know. You're genuine and you're from India!"

"Are you planning to experiment with someone from each country?" She brought out my playful sarcastic side, somehow.

"Haha not really, but…perhaps a few," she winked.

"You are crazy."

"I am. Hey, you know what I'm crazy for?" she asked with excitement.

"What?"

"Indian weddings. The groom comes in on an elephant!"

"Haha. It's not always an elephant, honey. Some grooms arrive in a fancy car, else mostly on a horse."

"I'm partial to the elephant. I also like all the ladies wearing heavy luxury costumes and shiny gold."

"Yup!"

"I would love to have a wedding like that. Let's get married once!"

"Once? How many times are you planning to get married?"

"Haha don't know. I haven't decided yet!" It felt strange having someone take life and relationships so lightly. After some casual banter, while caressing my chest softly, she slowly reached at my jeans.

"Are you a virgin?" she asked me abruptly.

"What do you think?" I asked, astonished at such a direct question. I guess I had to stop being surprised by this. It seemed to be the way here.

"Yes," she answered.

"Why do you think that?" I asked.

"Because you are Indian."

"So what?"

"People in India don't have sex before they get married."

"Looks like you've done some research! Traditionally yes, but that's not the norm these days. Things have changed with education and exposure. What about you?"

"Of course not," she said as if I'd accused her of murder.

"Eighteen?" I guessed.

"No, fifteen," she said.

"You are on fast forward!" When I was fifteen, just asking a beautiful girl to be my lab partner in science class was orgasmic. She took her hand to my zipper and said, with seduction in her eyes, "Mmmm… I wanna have some pipe."

"What?"

"Hehe, don't worry," she got up and went for her bag in the tent. She sat back down with a plunk, "This pipe, darling!" she said, as she pulled a small glass pipe from her bag.

"Hey, that's the same stuff we had at Terrell's party."

"Yup," she said, lighting it. Before she put her lips to it she said, "You talk sweet, you know. I like you."

I took two puffs and after a short while, the entire universe seemed to slow down, again. I felt as if I was flying, weightless, in the slow-moving clouds. My senses were ignited, and I could see, hear. I feel the splash of each wave, the chirp of each bird and every blink of her beautiful eyes. We moved to the tent, where we cuddled until the sun had dissolved into the arms of the horizon. We were so composed in tranquility that we never wanted the moment to end.

As the moon became the only light in the sky, she came even closer and whispered in my ear, "I have a gift for you."

I kept gazing at her, speechless. Wasn't this romantic evening gift enough?

She pulled something from her bag, and gently dropped it in my hand. The *right* moment had come. "*Just do it!*" She said in a subtle tone.

When we were finished, we started packing up our things and taking down the tent. After observing my slow movements she said, "Hey, are you alright?"

"Yeah, pretty much," and I gave her a soft kiss on the cheek.

Walking down, I was lost. I started walking away from her.

She couldn't understand my strange behavior. She asked, "Hey what happened?"

Silence…

"You wanna do this again sometime?" she asked with a playful wink.

"Not really," I said with some hesitation. She was surprised. And the pain of my long-distance relationship flashed back and hounded me all at once. I was standing on a thin line between an American beauty and my long-distance relationship. My passion took me to the beach but my conscience never wanted this to happen.

22

FREEDOM, AT A PRICE

On the brink of the second semester finals, I spent every waking hour studying and preparing. One night, I was up until 2 AM studying for the Financial Management final – a subject I was never quite able to manage. Needing a brain break, I got up to make a cup of coffee when I heard my phone ring. I picked it up and saw that it was Sonia. I felt a sudden jolt in my stomach. Guess something exciting to share. She never called me this late.

"Hey Soni," my voice filled with curiosity…

She was unable to speak. I heard only wailing and nose-blowing from her end of the conversation. I held my breath and said, "Soni, I am there with you, tell me what happened."

"Papa had a heart attack…"

"Oh Soni, I am so sorry. Are you okay? Where are you now?"

"We're at the hospital," she said, straining to speak through her tears. "The doctors took him to the ICU."

"What did they say?" No words…She was crying hard. "Soni, what did the doctor say? Tell me."

"He didn't say anything. He told us he'll let us know as soon as he knows anything. Karti I am so scared…I am…"

"Everything's going to be okay, Soni." I said softly, trying to calm her down. But of course I didn't know if everything was going to be okay.

"How did it happen?" I asked.

She spoke while crying, "I don't know. I was at the office and my mom called and asked to come home. When I asked her why, she said, 'Your dad can't breathe.' I nearly fainted, and Raghu brought me home. He brought us in his car to the hospital just in time. If we'd waited for an ambulance, who knows what might have…"

"Soni, he will be okay. He'll be okay."

Without saying a word she hung up the phone. I stood in the center of my room, not knowing what to do, completely helpless. The next moment I received a text message from Sonia: "I WISH you were here, I really need you right now."

I sat down on the chair and held my head in my hands. I really wanted to be there for (and with) Sonia. My old game of trying to make her believe that I was with her every moment had gone far too long, and didn't seem to mean much at that moment. In truth, I wasn't with her. I searched for flights that left for India the next day. The cheapest ticket I found was $2200. I logged into my bank account to check my balance. No surprise there, I had only $193 in my account.

JD returned from his late-night bay walk, saw me, and said, "You look like you've been hit by a truck. What happened jackass?"

I always shared everything with JD, even the most personal things I had on mind. He would share his philosophies on long-distance relationships and offer advice, and joke around with me. But in that moment, he was frozen too.

"Did you check for flights?" He asked.

"$2200."

"Okay, no problem, I have a thousand bucks. The rest I'm sure I can collect from the others. You just pack your bags," he said.

I nodded, overcome with emotion at his offer to help me. Then I remembered I couldn't possibly leave town. "What about the Financial Management and Market Research exams? They're this Monday and Wednesday!"

"Yeah, I know. You'll have to talk to the professors about that. How long do you think you'd be gone?" He asked.

"One or two weeks, I guess. Also, my family will contact me. They can't know that I am in India."

"Don't worry, I will handle the calls," JD said.

"Okay, let's book it." I opened my laptop and began filling out flight information. I began shaking, and I couldn't think of anything except getting on that flight and being with Sonia.

As I was about to finalize the airline ticket, JD jumped in. "Wait brother, I don't think you can go."

"Why not?"

"Because, since you're leaving the country, you have to get your Visa signed by the International Office. But it's closed on weekends."

"No way. I can't wait for three days. I can't…"

We went back and forth, processing the possibilities (and lack thereof) when finally JD sat on the couch and said, "*Bhai,* think about it. In three days, the situation might be better. She'll know more about how her dad is doing, and then you can make the call whether to go or not. Wait until Monday. If things haven't improved by then, you'll go."

I was stuck. Considering the circumstances, JD's advice was sound. But I was still torn. I was encircled by many unexpected limitations and all I wanted to do was get on a plane. I sat on the couch and the stillness really brought my attention to the situation. I began to cry. It had been all fun and games up till now, but in that moment it really hit me. Life was so simple when all I had to do was take the train from Ratlam to Indore. Had I been anywhere in India, it would have taken me just a few hours to reach Sonia, without the rigmarole of getting documents signed and other time-consuming formalities. I couldn't sleep all night. And I certainly couldn't study. I stared at the ceiling for hours, feeling guilty for not being there with Sonia; feeling guilty for enjoying my time on the beach with Jess; feeling guilty, somehow, for things I hadn't even done yet.

The next day I kept the phone with me at all times, waiting for an update from Sonia. I stared at it a few times, willing it to ring, but nothing. Finally I got a call from her. The doctor said that her father was out of danger now, but needed to be under observation for couple of days. I breathed for what felt like the first time that day.

"That's great, Soni. That is amazing news. I'm so glad he is okay." I jumped from the bed out of excitement.

"Hey…Thank you," she said, sounding a little distant.

"For what?" I asked. Did she know I had been up all night worrying about her? Did she know I had tried to book a flight but there were circumstances beyond my control that kept me from getting to her? I planned to tell her those things, but I hadn't told her yet.

"Go home now…" she said. I scrunched my face in confusion, and was about to ask her what she meant when she said, "Oh sorry, I was talking to Raghu. He's been staying at the hospital with me. He hasn't been home for two days."

I didn't have any words. I know I didn't have any right to be angry, but I was. Someone else was there with her, consoling her. It should have been me. But it wasn't, and I had no other choice but to accept it. That evening, JD came home and asked about Sonia's dad.

"He is out of danger now," I said.

"See, I told you. Now you may not need to go at all!" JD said happily, not noticing that I was upset.

How ironic that I was in a free country, but I was not actually free to do the things I wanted or needed to do, without having to jump through several hoops first. I did not make the decision lightly, but when I realized that my visit wouldn't make any difference anymore, I decided not to go. On Monday, the doctors discharged her dad. I was happy to hear that he had pulled through and would make a relatively speedy recovery, but I was heartbroken that I couldn't be there for her when she needed me most.

23

WHAT HAPPENS IN VEGAS,
STAYS IN VEGAS!

One evening, I was working out at The Harbor Point Gym, trying to exercise my whirlwind of thoughts away. I was a few minutes in to a treadmill workout for fifteen minutes when JD and Khanna rushed into the gym, grabbed my bag, and hit the emergency stop button on my treadmill.

"What the hell?" Leave it to them to ruin a guy's workout!

"Let's go," Khanna said, with an urgency I'd never seen in him before.

"Where? What happened?" I asked, worried I'd gotten a call from Sonia about her dad or something.

"Vegas, baby! Pack your bag," JD howled excitedly.

"Yo, baby!" cheered Khanna.

"Are you kidding me?" I couldn't afford to go to Vegas. They knew that.

"Listen, we just came across an online deal. It's only $400 for the flight *and* the hotel. It's a rare deal and we HAVE to take advantage of it," said Khanna.

"But… tomorrow? How can we go so soon?"

"Save your questions for the flight. Now let's go."

"Who else is going?" I asked.

"The three of us and Satya, of course," said JD. "Let's go!"

Easy for them to say. $400 was their monthly clubbing budget. I had to put that kind of money down as rent. But just as good friends help you out in tough times, they also put you in debt during the good times. It was a really good deal. A decent trip to Vegas usually averaged about $1000. It didn't take much arm-twisting. I packed my bags as told, and got ready for our adventure. Poor Satya too fell prey to their antics, and by early morning we were boarding a flight to the craziest destination ever.

On the plane, I pulled the in-flight magazine from the seat pocket in front of me. There was an article about Las Vegas – a destination like no other. I found it interesting and started reading aloud to my roomies:

"The emotional bond between Las Vegas and its customers is freedom. Freedom to do things, see things, eat things, wear things, and feel things we may deny ourselves in everyday life. Vegas give you the freedom to be someone you wouldn't (or couldn't) be at home. Have at it! *What happens in Vegas…Stays in Vegas!*"

I wasn't sure I'd do anything to take advantage of this mantra, but I was glad it was as it was, all the same.

When we landed in Vegas, we saw a huge billboard near the exit of the airport that said:

"Welcome to the *Fabulous* Las Vegas

The Universal Capital of Entertainment!"

Photo op! JD shot and uploaded the picture to Facebook with the caption: "Live Hard, Party Harder. That's Vegas, Baby!"

We took a bus from the airport that dropped us right in the center of The Strip. We were amazed to see the gigantic resorts and lavish casinos. Despite the many photos I'd seen, seeing it in person was simply astonishing. The vastness of it all was mind-blowing. I felt like I was in a dream. Paris, Venice and New York City's mirrors were a stone's throw away from each other and there were no rules. Sin City, indeed.

The best part of our deal was that it included three nights at the so-called queen of the The Strip - The Bellagio – the most lavish of all the resorts. The lobby alone looked like a grand kingdom. The corridors were lined with plush red carpets, and the railings were adorned with gold. It was really gold-plated aluminum, but who cared? When we entered the room, the first thing I saw was the bathroom, which was bigger and more luxurious than our entire Harbor Point apartment. The room itself was fit for a king. We jumped with arms wide open on the bed, welcoming any and all experiences that came our way on this trip.

Satya drew back the curtains and we were almost blinded by all the flashing lights outside. "Guys, what's the plan now?" he asked, as he gazed longingly down onto The Strip.

"Casino!" Khanna exclaimed, as he reached for his wallet.

"Clubbing!" countered JD.

"Adult show!" Khanna said, raising his wallet in the air.

"Strip club!" JD said, getting on board with Khanna's line of thinking.

"Oooh, maybe a massage first!" Khanna cooed. Satya and I just glanced at each other and laughed. So many things to do!

They spent so much time going back and forth about what to do first, by the time we left the hotel room it was already 9 PM. We hit The Strip like bulls unleashed. I noticed people walking down the street with drink buckets, canteens and other sorts of drinking apparatuses slung over their shoulders, happily reaching for a sip or swig as and when they pleased. I came to find out that in Vegas you could carry drinks on the street. Those drinking vessels were filled with beer. Woah! Every twenty steps or so, there were buskers playing music, young kids dancing, and others people and small groups performing various acts. I walked past a performer; entranced by her beautiful voice, I was taken by surprise when two hot girls in bikinis rushed to me and put their arms around my neck and shoulders. One of them asked: "How are you, handsome?"

"Good!" I said, rather confused but completely loving the whole situation. "How are you?"

"We are great. Would you like to take a photo with us?" She fluttered her eyelashes.

I didn't think I was so handsome as to attract such sexy girls who'd ask to take a photo with me, but I accepted it as my fate. I gave my camera to Satya (whom I treated as my official photographer on this trip) and, with a beer bucket hanging from my shoulder, I happily stood in between the two hot girls in bikinis holding their waists as they clung to me for the photo shoot.

"Hey friends, I can share these pictures if you want to give me your mobile numbers…" I said in a ploy to get their contact info and possibly date one of them.

They gave each other a strange look and said, "Sorry, we don't have our phones with us."

JD came to my side and whispered, "Dude, are you fucking Brad Pitt?"

"What do you mean?"

"Give them a tip."

"For taking that photo? But they're the ones who asked *me*…to be…in a photo…"

"You roadside loafer, do you really think you're that handsome? Fucker, now lose your pocket!" JD murmured.

I had $10, which I gave them. Khanna, JD and Satya laughed their butts off. Bastards. As we moved on, there were two guys distributing postcards. We took the postcards with disinterest and I was about to throw them away when I saw that it was a picture of a nude girl with her phone number written on it. The caption said, *"For a good time, call me now!"* JD and I looked at each other and quietly pocketed the cards.

About a half an hour later, I checked my mobile – seven notifications on Facebook! The first notification stated **"Khanna tagged you in a photo,"** with the enticing caption "Vegas Baby!" It was, of course, the photo of me with those two girls in bikinis! My jaw dropped as I clicked on the notification and saw more than 40 likes. Within thirty minutes! But the excitement was shot dead with the first comment. "Thanks for the gift! Bye!" Sonia had written. Fuck! Sonia!

I immediately deleted the photo. Boiling with anger at Khanna, I grabbed his collar and shouted, "You motherfucker!" and gave him a little shove.

"Hey, sorry *dost*! I really didn't think of this!" He staggered for a bit but found his footing. I shoved him again.

"You should have told me before tagging, *bhencho*."

"Sorry *yaa* but honestly I just forgot about Sonia."

"Fuck you!" I said, and immediately called her. She didn't answer. I could sense that she was terribly hurt by my immature act. I kept trying her number, every few minutes for a half an hour but I got no answer. After my umpteenth try, a message popped up. Sonia.

"First you left me for your ambitions, and now you have ditched me for your pleasures too. You can't imagine my struggle. Every day. I don't express it, because I don't want to worry you, but I am completely crushed under my responsibilities. My job is really hectic and extremely challenging, and on top of that, my dad hasn't recovered yet. At the end of each day I think of you, but I don't find you anywhere with me. You have left me stranded,

in the middle of nowhere. You are nothing but a tag of partner that I carry with me every day. I can't do it anymore. Please leave me alone, for God's sake."

This shook me up. The Vegas shine suddenly seemed uglier than darkness. I lowered my head and stared at my phone, not knowing what to do.

"*Bhai,* don't worry. Call her tomorrow and explain everything. She will be fine." JD tried to placate my anger.

"Is there anything left to explain now? Bastard Khanna."

"Okay, *bhai,* relax! You can't do anything about it now, especially if she won't take your call. Let's have some fun. You'll take care of it tomorrow!" He looked at me and said: "C'mon, it's Vegas baby!"

I felt so helpless in that moment, and I couldn't get my mind off of Sonia and what she thought I had done to her. Still, I tried to go with the flow with an absent mind. The flow brought us to a casino in Caesars's Palace – a massive resort on The Strip. As we entered the billowing palace, Satya leaned over and said softly, "Hey, have you ever been to a casino?"

"Yeah, every weekend in Ratlam," I gave him a cold reply. "Seriously, though. No. Never."

"Me neither," Satya said, and he seemed nervous about being *casino de-virginized* in this moment. I patted him on the back and gave him a look to suggest that we were in this together. It seemed to calm him.

Since we'd never gambled before, all the tables were new to us. JD and Khanna had to walk us through each game, and the different tables within that game. The most crowded tables were Blackjack, Roulette and Poker. Khanna grabbed an open spot at a Black jack table, and JD asked me and Satya to come play Roulette with him. Khanna was already so focused on his game, he didn't seem to notice that we left him to his own devices at the Blackjack table.

The Roulette table looked quite complex at first glance, but JD quickly explained the basic rules: bet on a color (black or red), and if the wheel stops on *any* number in that color, you win. The dealer was a young, beautiful girl and there were four other players sitting next to us. I did a quick tally and thought surely they each had about $1000 worth of chips in front of them; more than I had in all my bank accounts combined! Some people were betting $500 with every spin of the wheel, which was my grocery budget for three months. JD put $200 cash on the table and the lady gave him chips in return.

After eight or nine bets, JD won over $600. Being a *baniya*, I knew about earning profits, but I'd never seen a return of 200% in such a short span of time. I reached into my wallet, took out $60 cash and (filled with hope and a little bit of greed) put it on the table. The dealer looked at me as if I had entered a royal wedding in bathroom slippers, but she gave me my $60 worth of chips all the same. I tried my luck by putting $15 on my favorite color: black. I prayed to all the known Gods and Goddesses I could think of as the wheel went round and round. The ball stopped on 13 red. I lost. I put $15 more on black. The ball stopped on red. I lost again, but was distracted by a gorgeous cocktail waitress who'd come over with a tray of variety drinks and beer. I grabbed a beer and asked, "How much?"

"It's free, sir!" she replied with a huge smile. *Really?* Wow. I suddenly forgot about my $30 loss and placed a third bet of $15 on red. The ball stopped on black. I was totally annoyed. How is this happening to me? I had only $15 left. One more bet. *Black or red? Black or red?* I put it back on black and…I won! It went on like this for about an hour, winning some and losing others. But my bets were small and, like all gamblers everywhere, I eventually lost everything. Unable to face loss of $60, I put $60 more, thinking I could make up for the loss. Well, that backfired. Again I played for about an hour, and again I ended up losing everything. So, now I was out of cash! Satya, who'd entered the game as well, lost $100. No surprise there. The house always wins, as they say.

It was now 6 AM. Khanna had had enough of Blackjack and joined us.

"How much?" asked JD.

Khanna, with a disappointed expression, said, "I'm down $650."

Shit! I suddenly felt better about my loss - $120 was better than $650 any day.

"How about you, *Sindhi?*" asked Khanna

"How can someone pull money out of *Sindhi's* pocket?" Satya mocked.

"What's your secret?" I asked JD.

"There is no secret for victory here but had I been on your place, I would remember three things. One, keep a fixed budget. Two, never expect to earn money and three, consider the lost money as an entertainment cost – what you'd pay for movies and clubs; consider the amount you win as a bonus. That made sense. I spent $120 for a few hours of entertainment. I could live with that.

THE BOILER ROOM

It was the evening of our second day in Sin City. We had strolled from one casino to the next, wandered the streets with beer buckets hanging from our shoulders, chatted with cute girls, and eaten our fair share of indulgent hotel restaurant food.

"What next?" asked JD.

"Strip club," answered Khanna.

"Awesome." JD searched on his phone for a moment and then said, "The top-rated strip club is *The Thirst*"

"Well, I *am* thirsty!" Khanna said, with a look of satisfaction on his face. We hadn't even gotten to the strip club yet and he looked like he'd just bumped elbows with the most beautiful woman on earth.

Satya and I were happy to go along with whatever the night had in store for us. It was like Disneyland for adults. Everything surprises you.

We dressed up in white shirts and black suits and headed out for a night on the town. We stood in front of our hotel, waiting for the cab, when a long black Limousine pulled up in front of us. Our eyes widened as the driver rolled down his window.

"You want a ride?" he asked.

"Yes! Any good strip clubs around here?" asked Khanna. I guess a second opinion never hurt.

"You'll want to go to *The Thirst*. I can give you a ride for free!" said the driver.

It never occurred to us that we could get a free ride in Las Vegas in a luxury car! Apparently drivers get a handsome subsidy from the clubs, so they're able to offer free rides to first-timers like us.

The car was fully loaded. Dim lights, surround sound, rich leather seats, and a full-stocked bar in the corner. We felt like kings. This was royal treatment.

We reached the club where a half-naked girl was pictured on a large screen. It was my first time at a strip club, and I totally had no idea what would happen inside. When I entered, I was completely astonished. There was a stage in the center of the room, surrounded by tables and plush couches. On stage, a stunningly exotic dancer wearing black lacy lingerie was making all kinds of seductive moves on a pole, while men showered her with cash. We joined them, waving our signals in the air and encouraging her on while she danced for the crowd.

At one point, this stunning beauty left her pole and made her way up to every horny face near the edge of the stage. She came crawling up to Khanna, who was sitting right next to me. She held his face and surrounded it with her huge melons. I simply could not WAIT for my turn to come. Pleased, Khanna inserted $5 into her panty knot. She turned and caught my eye, and began crawling towards me. Then she lay down with her legs facing me, and stretched them out and apart. Oh my god! That was sensational! She slowly crept further down to me, held my face and enveloped it in her surprisingly soft bazoombas. *Jerks are those who go to the Grand Canyon.* But that wasn't all.

She then turned her sexy butt towards me and waited. Then I realized it was my turn to pay! As there was no price list for her tasks, I inserted $2. It was certainly worth more, but I had to tend to my budget.

After sometime, we grabbed a table and ordered our drinks. A stripper came to Khanna and sat on his lap. She placed her arms on his shoulder and leaned in for close conversation. I had never seen such intimacy! It looked as if they were celebrating their wedding night. After a while she held his hand and took him into a room called *The Boiler Room.*

I stared at the door of *The Boiler Room* with my mouth agape.

"What's happening? What are you staring at?" asked JD.

"What happens in there?" I asked, unable to peel my eyes away from the possibilities.

"Lap Dance," he said with a mischievous smile. And thus a new word was added to my US-English dictionary.

Just as I was mulling this new word over in my mind, a hot stripper came over and sat on *my* lap. I was aroused and went speechless.

Moving her index finger up and down my neck she whispered, "How are you, honey?"

I swallowed hard, trying to find my voice. "Fine," I finally said.

"You are so hot. I like you." she said, and she leaned in, just like Khanna's girl had. Now I was experiencing intimacy unlike any I'd known before.

"I like you too." My auto-generated response.

"What's your name?"

"KJ, what's yours?"

"I am Rosy."

"Pretty name," I said, not knowing what else to say.

"I think you want a lap dance." She winked.

I looked at JD, and he waved me on, silently. *Go!*

I nodded.

With a smile, she grabbed my hand and escorted me to the same mysterious *Boiler Room*. I was curious to see what happened inside. As we entered, there were several dark cubicles for personal lap dances. She took me to the last cubicle and tenderly pushed me onto the couch.

"Baby, you wanna go for one song or two?" she asked.

Looking at her curvaceous figure, I wanted to ask, "Is there an extended version? A full album, perhaps?"

She interrupted this thought as she said, "$20 for each song, honey."

Twenty bucks? Being a *Baniya*, I wondered if, perhaps, she'd do half a song.

Veiling my penny-pinching thoughts, I simply said: "One, please."

A new song came on, and she began moving sensually. She stood over me and bent at the waist, bringing her lips to my ear, inhaling and exhaling intensely with intermittent moans. Then she put one knee on the couch, held my waist with one hand, and gently caressed my chest with the other. Having been made aware of the rules, I was still and kept my hands to myself. Slowly she bent her other leg and placed her knee ever so gently on my (now extremely hard) joystick. This was intense!

Then, she did the most divine of all lap dance moves. She straddled me and sustained a grinding motion as I floated onto cloud nine. "Honey, one song is over!" I heard her say. "You want to continue?"

What? So fast? I was almost at my destination, and what stupid chump would arrive and not plant his flag?

"Keep going," I said, forgetting about money and intoxicated by the moment. When the second song was over, I was aroused beyond belief. And then it subsided. I gladly handed her $40. She deserved it.

The four of us reconvened at our table and ordered more drinks. We sat back and watched another stripper work that pole like nothing I'd ever seen, when a bouncer approached Khanna and said, "Sir, I need you to hand over your cell phone."

"Why?" Khanna asked, doing his best to look innocent.

"I saw you taking pictures, and it is strictly prohibited to use a camera inside the club."

"No, I wasn't using a camera," Khanna lied.

"Sorry sir, I'm going to need to check your cell phone." The bouncer held out his hand and Khanna reluctantly began handing it over. Impatient, the bouncer grabbed it before Khanna was ready to let it go, and he scrolled through twelve photos and three video clips Khanna had taken during our short time there.

"Sir, I'm gonna have to ask you to leave. You are in direct violation of the rules," he said in an authoritative tone, pointing us towards the door.

"But…"

"Sir, we can do this the easy way, or the hard way," and he flexed his muscles to show that he meant business. I felt like I was in a bad mobster movie. Then a wave of celebration ran through me as I realized this was his punishment for the Facebook offense.

Unfortunately it was my punishment, too. Khanna was thrown out of the club (it was pointless to argue with a 6'8" bouncer) and we all had to follow him out.

Back out on the street, Khanna asked, "How did they even know about the camera? It was hidden in my jacket."

"Cameras, dumbass." JD answered quickly. "Didn't you see there were cameras, like flies, all over the ceiling?"

"I will fuck him *up*. How dare he kick me out, *bhencho*…? He has no idea about my contacts in Delhi!" he said with an adamant political tone.

He kept shouting and we couldn't stop laughing. What an idiot. Like his contacts in Delhi could do anything for him. This was Vegas, baby!

24

OUR MOST AWAITED DAY

The ever-anticipated moment – going home for the first time since this adventure had begun – was on the horizon. We had had a fair share of fun in Vegas but going home seemed anticipatory in a whole new way. December was in full swing, and only one thing remained: final exams. And of course, shopping for loved ones.

I thought a Coach handbag would be perfect for my mom, even though the importance of the imprinted 'C' would surely be lost on her. And for my dad, an American bathrobe would be the perfect addition to his household wardrobe. Instead of appreciating it, however, I knew the first thing out of his mouth would be, "So damn expensive!" For Aditi, I would find outfits from *Forever 21*. I could just hear her saying, "This is okay, but what else do you have for me?" The ever-demanding little brat!

The two coolest brands – Abercrombie & Fitch and Hollister – T-Shirts for Vinay Chaddha, and my buddies Raghu and Kabeer.

It is well said that true love may break your heart, but you still love that person with every broken piece. This, truly, was how I felt about Sonia. After Vegas, things were never the same. Our contact and connection had fizzled out, but my feelings for her had not. Still, I had to respect her wishes and so instead of a romantic present, I got her a perfume gift-set from Victoria Secret. I hoped the gap between us would at least be filled with a gentle hug.

With shopping and exams done, the day to return had arrived. JD, Satya and Khanna had also packed their bags, and our luggage was lined up in the living room. Between the four of us, we had enough baggage to travel for a lifetime.

My flight to Mumbai was nineteen hours long, including a layover in London. This would be followed by a train ride to Ratlam. Before boarding, I updated my Facebook status.

"INDIA CALLING! Finally heading home after a year and a half away… WOOHOOO ☺☺☺ @Logan International Airport, Boston."

Everyone knew about my arrival except my sweet mom. The whole family had agreed that it would be the perfect surprise for her, and we were all anxiously awaiting her reaction to my arrival. After nineteen exhausting hours, I landed in the rich land of diversity, the land of my birth: India. Mumbai airport was dense with travelers and the noise level was above anything I'd heard in a long time. I loved it, because that's what I grew up with. I didn't necessarily miss it, being in Boston, but now that I was back it gave me a definite sense of comfort. There was a peculiar smell in the air that had an innate bond with my soul.

I reached the popular railway station in Mumbai: *Borivali Station.* It was spectacular to see the *Lifeline of Mumbai* – a rocket-speed Mumbai local train – overloaded with crowds of people, half of whom were hanging outside the train. Before boarding the Avanti Express to Ratlam, I ordered the signature dish of Mumbai - *Station VadaPav.* The first bite tickled my taste-buds as the bold spices and kick-you-in-the-ass garlic danced on my tongue. I was almost home.

I boarded the train to Ratlam. It forced me to hang my head out the window and feel the amazing wind on my face for the first time in eighteen months. The first ray of dawn shone when I was fifteen minutes away from my birthplace. I started recognizing the landscape, and began to count each breath as I came closer and closer to the town of my teenage years. As the train came to a halt, I heard, *"Chai, chai, garam chai."* It was no Starbucks, but it was comfortingly familiar. I stepped off the train and the world's best fragrance – delicious *Poha, Kachodi* and *Jalebi* – swept its way into my nostrils. I was home.

My family never bothered to greet me when I visited from Indore, but today after traveling for almost thirty-two hours, I saw that my entire family was there to receive me. My innocent mom was still lost as to why everyone had gotten together at the station, though I'm sure she had her suspicions. I took a deep breath, stepped off the train and flew, like a lost bird reuniting with his flock, into the arms of my family.

My mom nearly burst out in a bout of massive surprise. "OH MY SON, Kartik!" She launched herself at me, threw her arms around my waist and the first thing she said, with a choked voice, was, "You've gotten so thin!" In actuality, I had put on weight due to carelessly gobbling cheeseburgers and pizzas. Clearly, there are God-given filters for a mother's eyes.

My dad was next. I touched his feet, "Papa." Not only did he give me blessings, but he hugged me as well. That had never happened before.

Aditi hugged me with the same thrust with which she would fight with me, "Hey *bhai*, you have gotten so fair!"

"Oh really?"

"Your accent has also changed!" she said, looking at me with suspicious eyes. Same old Aditi.

A flood of happiness ran through my veins. Yes, these are the three changes – health, skin-tone and accent – that close ones keenly observe upon your first-in-a-long-time visit to India from abroad.

During the short car ride home, I couldn't stop gazing out the window. I entered the nostalgic world of Ratlam. There were the same old faces in the same old roadside tea stalls, the same animals roaming the streets, the same potholes and speed bumps. Nothing had changed – except, perhaps, me (and my exposure to a larger city). Ratlam looked so small after eighteen months.

Finally, we reached our street and my own home came into view. My heart leaped with joy. Though the colors seemed faded, and a few dry garlands and lights from *Diwali* were still hanging, there was something fresh and new about it. Perhaps it was my own perspective. The one thing that remained constant was Gupta*ji*. He was, as usual, sitting on his porch. He jumped

"Namaste, Namaste bete! Come in!" I politely told him I would see him later. When I finally entered my house, I prayed to the Lord Krishna idol – this was more to appease my dad – and then settled into my favorite place in the house: the kitchen.

I was going to be there only for twenty-six days, they had already filled up my schedule, and without my consent. Everyone wanted me to spend time with them: my relatives, all my neighbors, Aditi's friends, etc. My mom made it clear that I had to make it a priority to be around her as much as was possible.

But there would certainly be a tradeoff; I would have to make time for my sin partners Raghu and Kabeer. And of course for my lost love Sonia. I hoped I'd be able to spend one day with her. Just one day after eighteen months of absence, but that's all I could afford. I was apprehensive about meeting Raghu because I didn't want my intuitions to come true. I tried to contact him several times but he never responded.

It was breakfast time.

"You know what?" I asked Aditi the next morning, as we drank our tea together in the drawing room.

"What?"

"Happiness is being home after eighteen months!" She laughed and gave me a playful punch in the arm, as if to say *we're happy you're home, too.* I enjoyed the experience of surprising my family with the gifts I had gotten them but I am sure my Dad was calculating every penny spent as his face went sullen every time I pulled out a gift.

The next day, I got a message from Kabeer. I packed a bag with gifts and chocolates and headed out the very next morning for Indore.

The moment I came out of the station, I spotted Kabeer. He was hard to miss, with his long beard, folded sleeves and wrinkled shirt. He pulled me in for a tight hug. It was great to see him!

"Hey, *Ratlami!* You've gotten so fair!" He said with surprise. It was the first thing everyone noticed. Funny!

We walked through the parking lot, and he stopped at a shiny new car in the parking lot. I thought it was a joke. "Don't tell me this is your car." He jiggled the keys playfully and unlocked the door.

"Where are we heading?" I asked, as I lowered myself into the comfy leather seat.

"Guess!"

"*JPC?*"

"YES!" I jumped out of my seat. That used to be one of our favorite hangouts.

We hit *JPC*, which stood for *Joshi Poha Center*, owned by Murli Joshi. He was a short, mustached man in his mid-forties, who we referred to as Murli *Kaka* (uncle). It was a typical breakfast spot with two rustic benches in a corner. In addition to selling delicious food like *Poha* and *Kachodi*, he had cigarettes and tobacco. As soon as Murli *Kaka* saw me, he left the tea he was making and ran over to me, excited, "*Oh ho! Kartik bhaiya!* Welcome welcome! After so long!"

"*Namaste* Murli Kaka, How are you?"

"All fine, where are you?"

"I am in the US, Kaka."

"Oh my God, how wonderful!" He yelled out to one of his workers, "*Ae chhotu chai lana malai maar ke*" (bring three mugs of tea with cream). I knew I was in for a treat.

"So what does the US look like?" he asked.

"Heaven, *Kaka*, Heaven!"

"Are there any heavenly tea stalls, like this one?" he asked, only half-joking.

"No, Kaka." I laughed, "We have big coffee shops, like Starbucks."

"I remember those days when you three would come every day…" he said, emotionally. I remembered those times, too. They were the good old days, indeed.

When we had finished our tea and snacks, I asked, "How much do we owe you, *Kaka*?"

He kept his hand on my shoulder and said, "Kartik *bhaiya*, you have changed."

"What do you mean, *Kaka*?"

"You never used to pay on time." We all laughed.

True to fashion, he didn't take a single penny from us that day. "It's on the house," he said. The bond I had with Murli *Kaka*, as evidenced by his generosity that day, was something I had not been able to cultivate in the US, yet.

Kabeer and I grabbed our favorite table aligned next to *JPC*. After a minute of silence, I asked apprehensively, "Where is Raghu?"

"What else, tell me, how's US?" Kabeer tried to avoid the subject.

"I asked something!" My tone grew more serious and affirmative.

He was silent. After a long pause, he said, "Perhaps, you might not want to hear it."

My veins started to stretch. "Just tell me!"

Kabeer explained, "After you went to the US, he met Sonia several times as her life was left with some sort of vacuum. Gradually, he started falling for her. Sonia was apprehensive towards their closeness at the same time she was not able to digest that you literally left her for your dreams. However, she was completely changed after her father's incident. She does not know what she wants now."

"What?" I asked, sounding surprised despite realizing the truth.

"You know what I mean, brother." He patted my back.

I was flitting between anger and regret: anger for Raghu's dishonesty and regret of my going to the US. Even I didn't know what was right.

Listening to all this made me desperately want to meet Sonia. She knew I was coming to India at some point in December, but she never bothered to ask about the details of my visit. I was constantly swinging between love, hurt and a bruised ego. Now I wanted to get back at Sonia more than ever and the only way was to meet and please her. I finally decided to send her a Facebook message, trying to appeal to her soft side. "Soni, I am in Indore. You may not want to see me, but I will still be waiting for you at *Shake & Bake* – our second home – at 5 PM on Tuesday."

I arrived at *Shake & Bake* early by thirty minutes. That never used to happen.

After a long and agonizing wait, I heard a sweet voice call out, "Kartik?" There she was! Standing next to me, at last! I jumped up and hugged her, "Sonnni!" She seemed dazed as she held me. Without saying anything, she sat in the seat across me. Her eyes darted about as she avoided eye contact with me at all cost. I had to find a way to break the ice; a way to get through to her and at least get her to look me in the eye again.

"I brought you your favorite chocolates from Boston – the ones that you always asked for!" I slid them across the table gently, hoping I'd catch her eye and show her how sorry I was about everything.

"Thanks," she said, as she took the chocolates, still avoiding eye contact.

"I also got you a perfume set. It's V.S., Your favorite brand..." I gave her the beautifully wrapped perfume gift-set. She was quiet and kept averting her eyes while presenting a stoically expressionless face.

"Soni, look at me. I am here...with you," I said, emotionally.

No response.

"Okay, look at me. I'm here. Can we just...connect now and forget the past?"

She looked at me for the first time that evening and said, "Can you give me something if I ask you for it?"

"Sure, Soni, anything for you!" I replied, confidently. "Can you give me back time? Can you take away the tough times I faced, the struggles I encountered, the pain I buried deep within, and the hurdles I jumped all by myself while you were off gallivanting in America?"

"You weren't all by yourself," I rebutted, but she wouldn't have it.

"That is bullshit and you know it!"

With a fragile look I said, "You have changed, Soni."

"I never wanted to, but *you* brought me to this!"

"What are you talking about? You never said anything to me. You were always silent during our calls. You never wanted to share what was going on with you." She was speechless. "I want to know one thing," I continued, trying to catch her eye, "Are you in love with someone else?" I asked, despite not wanting to hear the painful truth.

She trembled and went silent. Tears fell from her eyes. I was waiting for her answer, feeling immensely hurt by her silence. Suddenly, her phone rang, and the name that flashed on the screen was "LoveRag."

My blood boiled with anger, I yelled, "You ditched me!"

She wasn't buying it, she responded with equal thrust, "You brought this to happen, Okay!"

She started crying, holding her cell phone like it held all the answers. The same tears that encouraged me to fall in love, were now insisting that it was time to move on. I looked at *Shake & Bake* for the last time and left. All the beautiful memories flashed back in that single moment as my throat choked and my eyes filled with tears. Indore became colorless. I did not try to contact Raghu because the friendship was not possible anymore. Even if I fought to get Sonia back, I wouldn't get the same love from her. The truth was that I lost a close friend whom I trusted more than myself, and a true love who taught me how to be trustworthy. The day was a nightmare for me.

When leaving Indore, my heart was completely drowned in tears with two questions: *Should I have NOT gone to the US?* Or if *betrayal by my brother-like friend and my soul-mate was a rightful act?*

In the blink of an eye, twenty-six days had gone by. They ended with a mother's tears and a father's iron-fisted warnings. As I sat on my long flight to Boston, I realized that they no longer had a say in what I did. With the extreme altitude – miles above the earth – came the sinking feeling that I had lost something important and by returning to the States to finish my education, it would be lost forever.

25

THE PROUD MOMENT

One week after returning from India, I found myself feeling more doleful than ever before. Leaving family and friends again was gloomy enough, and the interaction with Sonia completely shattered me. My depression reached pretty alarming levels, and I realized that I really needed to share my grief with someone. Jess was someone I hoped would be there to give me a shoulder. I felt like calling her but my conscience stopped me because of the "emotional turmoil" in my life that had ruptured my trust on anyone. I realized, perhaps the biggest truth of life is that *life doesn't always go the way you want.* Something will be lost beyond recall.

Graduation came with a flood of new responsibilities and experiences. By the last semester, our priorities were narrowed down to include just one thing: getting a full-time job. Having a full-time job after graduation becomes inevitable for most students for many reasons including paying off student loans, and to discharge family and societal expectations. So, I earnestly began to look for jobs.

Time seemed to be moving faster than ever. Classes flew by. The job search compounded my routine greatly. It felt like I had only just begun, when Graduation Day arrived. I was given a black cap and gown which I wore with utmost pride as I did the 'Grad Walk.' The crowd burst with applause as each student walked up to accept his or her diploma from the Dean.

Two of my close friends, Natasha and Khanna, had their parents in the audience, which made me miss my family. The most anticipated moment of the ceremony had arrived – we stood in a large cluster and made eye contact with everyone around us. In an almost silent agreement, we bobbed, counted, and in perfect synchrony, we threw our caps up in the air. Within moments, most of us had updated our Facebook statuses as well. JD, Satya, Khanna and I scurried home after the festivities to set up our own grand celebration. We decorated the kitchen with bottles of liquor, leaving very little space for anything else. People began to arrive early in the evening, and within just a few moments, it seemed as if everyone was far drunker than I'd ever seen them before. Even Shalini, who never had more than one glass of wine, was completely sloshed. From GMAT to Graduation was a full three-year struggle. We deserved this party, and everyone deserved to be as drunk as they wanted to be. This was a huge accomplishment.

When the party was over in the wee hours of the morning, I stumbled into my room, half-conscious, and threw my cap down onto my pillow. I remembered that the pillowcase had been a gift from Sonia. As she gave it to me, she had kissed it and said, "No matter what happens, I will be there with you at the end of each day." Though we started this journey together, I never imagined finishing it alone.

The next day, I woke up with a new sense of purpose. Suddenly, student life in the US felt like a vacation. I knew I had to put my entrepreneurial dreams on the backburner and look for a 'real' job for now — what with a hefty loan and the endless weight of family pressure. I had no other choice.

I wasn't alone. Satya, Shalini, Natasha and JD also felt the pressure too quickly find a lucrative full-time job. Khanna, on the other hand, returned to India to join his dad's business.

The real struggle started with the first job application. "Thank you for applying for the position. We regret to inform you that your skills do not match our requirements." I found this sentence very often in my inbox, I had a mind to give up and return to India with my tail between my legs. Or, at the very least, to look for a part-time job at a restaurant or gas station, or somewhere that might pay the bills and allow me to survive the winter.

The main threat as time wore on was not making the deadline. Yes, there was a deadline to leave the US and that was just a year after graduation. In mid-February a financial firm based in New York called me for an interview. I spent the days leading up to the interview clearing my head, and imagining myself already having the job. I was going to land a full-time job even if it killed me. I returned to Boston, feeling pretty good about the interview, and I hadn't even stepped into my apartment when a call came in, offering me the job. OH MY GOD! This was a dream come true! NEW YORK CITY!

I had successfully completed the last lap of my career marathon thanks to my mentor, Ron, who recommended me for a position. Ah, the merits of networking are endless!

I realized that leaving Boston was as tough as leaving Ratlam. On my last night in Boston, JD, Satya, Shalini, Natasha and I sat together with our beloved hookah, recalling our best moments in the past, and celebrating the possibilities for my future in NYC. JD and Shalini had both gotten jobs in Boston, so I guess it *was* meant to be, after all. Natasha accepted an offer from a pharmaceutical company in Los Angeles, California, and Satya was still waiting to hear back, but he was hopeful. The celebration lasted till the morning. But the time had come when I had to make the drive to New York. Moving out of Harbor Point left a bit of a hole in my heart, but the 'Big Apple' would surely fill the emptiness.

26

THE PURSUIT OF HAPPINESS

As I walked from the subway to my brand new, fancy adult job, memories of that New Year Eve flashed back, when Satya and I were posing for a photo shoot, pretending that we worked for the company whose name was on the billboard. The next thing I knew, I was entering that very same building, only this time, there was nothing to pretend.

An admin officer welcomed me, and showed me to my office. It was small, but luxurious, with two wide-screen monitors, custom-built, spit-shined furniture, and my very own letterhead, ready for my official use. As I was setting up my desk, personalizing the space a bit, a guy in his mid-thirties, in a grey suit and horn-rimmed, black, glasses stood at my door. "Kartik?" He asked, already seeming to know the answer.

"Yeah," I nodded.

"Hi, I'm Deepak, Deepak Rungta." He approached me with his hand outstretched.

"Hi Sir! Nice to meet you!" I said, as I shook his hand with as much strength as I could muster. I felt a sense of comfort to have an Indian manager.

He showed me around, introduced me to my team, and then took me to lunch where he described the company, its products, and the work culture in detail. I found myself conscious during the interaction.

I rented a room in New Jersey, which was an hour's commute to and from Manhattan. Two hours a day, I spent on public transportation, just to escape the exorbitantly high New York City expenses. I had done it for six months already. Those six months involved an exponential learning curve. My H1 (Job Visa) had been approved for three years. Each paycheck brought a smile to my lips, but the very next day, I'd watch the funds be taken away by the loan monsters. My priority over renting an expensive apartment in Manhattan, or buying a luxury car, was to get my student loans paid off as quickly as possible.

Six months into my new job in this new city, I found myself really missing my old friends. We were in touch on Facebook, but of course it was no more the same.

ONE YEAR LATER

A year had gone by so quickly, I almost couldn't believe it when JD reached out and scheduled a conference call for our "anniversary." By then, Satya had joined the workforce in Chicago.

One evening, I was having coffee with Deepak Rungta who had always been nice to me, so when he asked if I'd like to join him for coffee after work, I accepted.

"What's your plan for the future, Kartik?" he asked, blowing gently on his hot coffee.

"I plan to work in the US for two or three years, and I'll go back to India," I answered sincerely. That was, after all, my plan. It had been all along.

He laughed out loud.

"Why do you laugh?" I asked with a confused smile on my face.

"Come see me in three years," he answered.

"But I am serious. That's been my plan all along."

He laughed even harder.

Trying to maintain my smile, though I was growing more and more concerned, I asked, "Why are you laughing at me?"

"Hey relax. I am not laughing at *you*. I'm actually laughing at myself, if you can believe it." I gave him another skeptical look. "When I started here, my manager asked me the same question and you know what I said?"

"What?" I asked.

"Two to three years!" he again laughed.

"Why didn't you end up going back?" I asked.

"*NYC*."

"New York City?"

"No, it's what I call *Next Year Cycle*. After college, I thought: *I'll build savings and gain some experience. Then I'd go back*," Deepak began.

"Then?"

"With a good job in US, the marriage proposals started pouring in from India. I thought: *I'll get married first. Next year I'll go back.*" "And then?" My curiosity increased.

"I thought: *we'll just spend the honeymoon period here, and then we'll go back.*"

"And after the honeymoon?" My eyes and ears were getting broadened with each question.

"My wife got her Master's degree and started working. We were both earning well, and we decided to buy a house and build equity, rather than paying rent."

"So why didn't you just skip the house and go home?"

"We wanted to have a baby who would be a citizen of the US by birth. We thought: *we'll move next year; next year at the latest.* And so we bought the house."

"And then you had a baby?"

"Yep, and *then* we thought: *perhaps we should expose him to an American education. Two more years and then we'll go back.* And do you know how long it's been?"

"How long?"

"Ten years."

"Ohh"

"*NYC* is no joke. And now, after all this time, my green card should be arriving in about six months."

"Awesome!"

"Then I will return to India. *Next year.*" He looked at me, wondering if I'd gotten the joke. We both had a good laugh.

"Any advice on how to escape this cycle?"

"If you really want to go back, dive in when you have the least responsibilities. The longer you delay, the harder it is to leave."

"It's just that I *have* to save money now in order to start my business in India."

"Sure, but just know there is no threshold amount. You know, I have more debt now than I had when I was a student: home loans, car loans, education loans, and the list goes on. Expenses have trapped me here."

"So you mean if I don't take a step now, I will never be able to go back?" I asked with anxiety.

"I'm not saying it's impossible, you certainly *can*, but you have to remember one thing: in the course of saving money and more money, you lose sight of the most important thing."

"What's that?"

"*Passion!* Yes, that passion and urge to do something new. You settle into your comfort zone with your stable job and your family."

"Are you saying I should pack my bags and get out while I can?"

"No, I'm saying you might have to make a choice. Do you want to be happy, or do you want to be fulfilled? Living in the US is happiness. Living in India surrounded by family is fulfillment."

"That's simple, then. I choose fulfillment. Fulfillment is beyond happiness."

"Not necessarily. From experience, I can honestly say that living with CLARITY of the FUTURE is always better than living a life in constant doubt."

I wasn't sure what to make of all that. I felt like a five-year-old who'd been stranded on the playground. Only time would tell which way life would take me. I thanked Deepak for the coffee, stood up, picked a random direction and lifted my arms to the sky. *I'm open to whatever it is I'm supposed to do, or find, or become.* And with that thought, I boarded the train and headed home to Jersey.

A NEVER-ENDING CALL!

Aditi moved to Indore to pursue her Bachelor's degree. She didn't want to admit it, but she was following my footsteps.

Kabeer completed his M.Tech and became a lecturer at our college in Indore. He found it very difficult. Not the teaching part, the having-to-dress-decently part. A call from Raghu is still awaited. He never dared to contact me since the day I left India. And then there's Sonia, her prolonged silence had broken my trust forever. After this excruciating experience, I will never be the same Kartik again.

JD, Shalini, Satya, Natasha, and I got to conference often to smoke out the tensions of life. They were all doing well. JD and Shalini were still in Boston, Satya loved Chicago, and Natasha swore she would never live anywhere else – Los Angeles was her home now.

As for me, I remained content to take it one day at a time. After another year had passed, I was having lunch at work when I got a call from my mother, who was always worried about me for no good reason.

"Bete," she said, after a long emotional pause. "I miss you so much. When are you going to come back?"

I looked out of my office window at the vibrant city below me and thought for a moment. I said, "Next year, ma. Next year…"

– SHOULD I STAY OR GO BACK? –

www.ingramcontent.com/pod-product-compliance
Lightning Source LLC
Chambersburg PA
CBHW051437250726
48655CB00001B/114